super
soups

michael van straten

super soups

healing soups for mind, body, and soul

mitchell beazley

Dedication
In the most loving memory of my mother, Kitty: I'll always remember that wonderful aroma as I arrived home from school to see her making chicken soup.

An Hachette UK Company
www.hachette.co.uk

First published in Great Britain in 2002 by Mitchell Beazley, a division of Octopus Publishing Group Ltd, Carmelite House, 50 Victoria Embankment, London EC4Y 0DZ
www.octopusbooks.co.uk
www.octopusbooksusa.com

This revised and updated edition published in 2015

Copyright © Octopus Publishing Group Ltd 2015

Distributed in the US by Hachette Book Group, 1290 Avenue of the Americas, 4th and 5th Floors, New York, NY 10020

Distributed in Canada by Canadian Manda Group, 664 Annette St., Toronto, Ontario, Canada M6S 2C8

ISBN: 978-1-78472-096-4

Printed and bound in China

10 9 8 7 6 5 4 3 2 1

Publishing Director: Stephanie Jackson
Editor: Pollyanna Poulter
Deputy Art Director: Yasia Williams
Design and illustration: Grace Helmer
Photographer: Nicki Dowey
Production Controller: Sarah-Jayne Johnson
Index: Isobel McLean
Americanizer: Nicole Foster

contents

introduction 6

soup basics 8

immune-boosting soups 18

circulation soups 32

skin-reviving soups 46

sexy soups 58

restorative soups 72

slimming soups 86

good-mood soups 100

winter-warming soups 112

soup garnishes 124

soup healing 132

index 141

introduction

"It's good soup, and not fine words, that keeps me alive."
Molière, 1672

Just thinking of the word "soup" conjures up mental images of a family kitchen from bygone days: a huge pot bubbling on the stove, wonderful aromas wafting through the house, and the instant welling-up of happiness and appetite. All over the world, soup is basic food, and has been since the earliest recipes were documented. Long before there were written records, soups appeared in drawings and paintings. From the hearty, thick-enough-to-stand-a-spoon-in soups of northern and eastern Europe to the subtle, delicate flavors of Asia, soup has long been a staple food for almost every culture.

Fish soups from all over the Mediterranean, chowders from America, bean and pasta soups from Italy, traditional French onion soup, recipes adapted from former colonies (such as the Indian influence in mulligatawny)... these are not only wonderful dishes to eat, but they're healing dishes as well. Whether you want a substantial meal-in-a-bowl on a cold winter's evening or the most delicate, crystal-clear broth as an appetizing start to your light summer supper, the super soups in this book will fulfill the needs of both your taste buds and your health.

Some of the earliest written recipes come from the pen of the great Roman gourmet Apicius, thanks to whom we have the details of the culinary traditions of ancient Rome and Greece. More than 2000 years later, it is fascinating to discover that the cooks of the classical world were using cloves, ginger, cardamom, nutmeg, pepper, and cinnamon—and that they understood the medicinal value of these exotic spices. Maybe their Roman chicken broth was the forerunner of the now-famous "Jewish penicillin" (chicken soup), or perhaps the original version of my bean and barley soup could have been eaten by Julius Caesar, when it might have contained chickpeas, lentils, barley, leeks, cilantro, aniseed, fennel, oregano, lovage, and cabbage. Today, a bowl of super soup is still a welcome treat, whether hot and warming in winter or chilled and refreshing on a balmy summer's day. But if the only soup you have ever tasted comes out of a carton, a can or—heaven forbid—a packet of powder, you don't know what you're missing. If these are your staples as far as soup is concerned, you're certainly getting far too much salt (which will push up your blood pressure), probably spoonfuls of chemical additives, and definitely far less health-promoting nourishment than you would from any of the recipes included in this book.

Besides the obvious flavor and health benefits, nothing you do in the kitchen engenders the feeling of caring and loving as much as making soup. Paul McCartney once said that he'd rather have a bowl of his late wife Linda's soup than eat at the poshest restaurant in London. I agree with him about the soup—my wife Sally's soups certainly keep me at home. Many people are put off soup-making because they think it's too complicated. Let me assure you: nothing is simpler than super soup-making. It's quick, easy, and can be incredibly inexpensive besides. In terms of nutritional value for money, homemade soup must be the best of all health bargains. Not only do you get a bowlful of protective vitamins and minerals, body-building protein, and energy-giving complex carbohydrates, but you also benefit from enzymes and plant chemicals that improve digestion, boost resistance, and fight off infections.

So don't waste a minute: go to the stores now, then get into the kitchen and start cooking. All the recipes serve four people. Once you've tasted the results of these deliciously simple super soup recipes, you'll soon become a dedicated soup-maker—and a promoter of good health into the bargain.

soup basics

the soup-maker's kitchen **10**

stock basics **12**

vegetable stock **13**

fish stock **14**

chicken stock **15**

ham stock **16**

beef stock **17**

the soup-maker's kitchen

For some reason I've never understood, soup-making seems to have acquired the mystical qualities of Macbeth's three witches. Believe me: you don't need a coven or strange parts of unspeakable animals to make great soups. What you do need are good-quality ingredients, a chopping board, sharp knives, and a decent, heavy saucepan. Amazing machines can make the process easier, but you can still make wonderful soup without them.

the pantry

My friend the great chef Raymond Blanc told me that with two carrots, an onion, and a few fresh herbs, he could make a soup fit for a king. And it's true: the beauty of soup-making is that you can use practically anything to create delicious results. The Brussels sprouts and Stilton left over the day after Christmas, what's left of your roast chicken, the outer leaves of a cabbage, that parsnip you didn't get around to using, a half-empty bag of frozen peas, even the bell peppers left over from a salad... you can use them all.

In order to make the best use of such leftovers, however, you do need to keep some staple items on hand. Essentials include a few cans of beans, tomatoes and chickpeas, tomato paste, some packages of lentils, red and yellow split peas, a tub of low-salt, organic vegetable and herb granules, and finally, yeast and herb extract—the Swiss-made Bioforce and Marigold brands are the best. Herbs are essential, too, and fresh are definitely best. If you grow your own, most can be frozen in ice-cube trays and added as required, but do keep a supply of dried bouquets garnis, sage, thyme, bay, oregano, *fines herbes*, chilies, and your other favorites on hand. Keep some fresh garlic and onions in your pantry as well.

gadgets

If you're serious about soup, it's worth buying a decent stockpot with a basket; otherwise, you'll need a big, fine-meshed strainer. Blenders make soup-making easier and quicker, and they needn't cost the earth. An immersion blender costs around $30.

If you have more money available, choose from a wide variety of standard blenders.

The best is undoubtedly the American-made KitchenAid (although it is also the most expensive). Another really good gadget is the hand-held Bamix. Swiss engineering makes this a chopper, blender, mixer, and grinder that will also puree soup. At around $200, it's not cheap—but it is very popular with professional chefs.

The best gadget of all is the German Thermomix. This is a combined food processor, cooker, and steamer with which you can make fabulous soup, all in one container, from start to finish. It will also make jam in twenty minutes, sorbets in two, and bread dough, batter and sauces at the push of a couple of buttons. It does cost around $1500, but if you're a serious cook, it will last a lifetime and give you endless pleasure.

When it comes to knives, chopping boards, and other cooking paraphernalia, the best value for money (and widest selection) I've found comes from Lakeland Limited, which has a good internet site (www.lakelandlimited.com). I've tried most brands of knives on the market, but those that are head and shoulders above the rest are made in Japan by NipponKitchen. They hold their edges much longer than other knives. If you want the best, then these are certainly worth the money.

stock basics

Most people believe that they don't have enough time to make simple soups, let alone the time to make stock. While it is true that making your own stocks can be time-consuming, believe me, it is worth the effort. Of course, you can use the ever-popular bouillon cubes, but generally they contain far too much salt and a wide range of chemical preservatives, flavorings, colorings, and hydrogenated fats that you and your family would be better off without. Happily, organic varieties are now available—there are even some low-salt, organic products, too. So if you must use a bouillon cube for convenience, choose the healthier options from health-food stores or supermarket shelves.

In the convenience world of the 21st century, it is also possible to buy "fresh" stock alongside the "fresh" cartons of soup in most supermarkets. These are certainly an improvement on stock cubes and powdered or canned soups, but they are extremely expensive, still far too salty, and not a patch on the genuine article that you can easily make in the most basic of kitchens. After all, it's not so long since our ancestors did it all in an iron pot on a cooking range fueled with wood or coal. You can use bouillon cubes or cartoned stock for all the recipes in this book, but if you want your super soups to have the maximum health-giving impact, good homemade stock is fundamental.

The reason? Even the healthiest and best of the available instant products lack the nutritional quality and flavor that come from using homemade stock, so if you do nothing else with this book, at least try the vegetable stock recipe on page 13; it couldn't be simpler. Take a few hours to brew up a giant potful, then concentrate it by boiling it down to half its volume. Once it has cooled, freeze it in ice-cube trays, then empty the cubes into a double freezer bag, making sure to label and date it. You can keep liquid stock in the fridge for a couple of weeks, or in the freezer for a couple of months.

When you need the stock for soups, sauces, or gravies, use each cube with the same amount of water. A rough guide is half-a-dozen cubes in a casserole or stew, a couple with the vegetable water to make gravy, three or four with boiling water for risotto, or as many as you need to make up the stock for the following recipes. You can do exactly the same with chicken, beef, fish, and ham stocks to bring back the traditional flavor and health-giving benefits of the stockpot to your kitchen.

The stock recipes on the following pages are my own personal favorites.

the healthiest base for most super soup recipes
vegetable stock

When I was a child, mothers, grandmothers, and elderly relatives insisted that children drink the vegetable cooking water (I know mine all did): not a drop was ever wasted, as all of it went into soups, sauces, gravies, and casseroles. As with many old wives' tales, there was sound reasoning behind this practice: the cooking water is nutrient-rich, containing vitamins, minerals, and enzymes leached out of the vegetables during the boiling process.

2 onions, 1 quartered, 1 left whole with the skin on

3 large celery sticks

2 large carrots, coarsely sliced

1 large leek, sliced

1 large parsnip, chopped

1 large sprig of sage

2 sprigs of thyme

6 bay leaves

1 small bunch of parsley

about 4 cups water

8 black peppercorns

½ teaspoon salt

Put all the ingredients into a large saucepan—or ideally, a pasta pan with a fitted strainer.

Bring slowly to a boil.

Simmer for about 1 hour.

Remove the pasta strainer or strain through kitchen cheesecloth or a strainer, pressing the vegetable pulp with a wooden spoon to extract maximum liquid.

for all-over protection and good digestion; essential in fish cookery
fish stock

Homemade fish stock tastes absolutely stunning and will impart a uniquely professional flavor to all fish and shellfish soups, sauces, and risottos. It is rich in iodine, a mineral often deficient in modern diets and essential for the normal function of the thyroid gland. The protective benefits of onions and leeks, combined with the digestion-improving essential oils from mint and tarragon, make this a healthy base for all your fish cookery.

3½oz fish trimmings and bones (most supermarkets offering a filleting service will keep trimmings if given a day's notice)

3 carrots, cubed

2 sweet, white Spanish onions, peeled and coarsely chopped

1 large leek, coarsely chopped

1 large sprig of rosemary

1 bunch of parsley

1 bunch of mint

3 large sprigs of tarragon

6 cups water, or 14 cups water and 2 cups dry white wine

8 white peppercorns

½ teaspoon salt

Put the washed and dried fish trimmings in a large saucepan.

Add the rest of the ingredients and bring slowly to a boil.

Simmer for about 30 minutes, skimming the surface regularly.

Strain through kitchen cheesecloth or a fine strainer.

an all-round stock with plenty of vitamins
chicken stock

After vegetable stock, this is probably the most useful stock recipe. Because it's fairly neutral in flavor, good chicken stock can be substituted for beef or ham stock. It is particularly good for making most soups and risottos, and is perfectly acceptable as the base for most sauces and gravies—unless, of course, you're cooking for vegetarians.

A good chicken stock is a valuable source of enzymes and B vitamins, as well as the mood-enhancing essential oils found in rosemary and sage, and the protective plant chemicals found in onions, leeks, thyme, and bay leaves.

1 chicken carcass (your butcher may sell them; otherwise, do it yourself or use the bones from roast chicken)

2 quarts water

6 scallions

1 large leek, coarsely chopped

2 large celery sticks, chopped

1 large sprig of rosemary

½ large bunch of parsley

1 large sprig of sage

2 large sprigs of thyme

3 bay leaves

10 white peppercorns

about ⅓ teaspoon salt

Put the chicken carcass in a large saucepan. Cover with the water.

Bring to a boil and simmer for about 30 minutes.

Add the rest of the ingredients.

Bring back to a boil and simmer for 40 minutes.

Strain through kitchen cheesecloth or a strainer.

the digestible choice for pork-based soups

ham stock

The robust flavor of ham stock is perfect for recipes such as Dutch pea soup with smoked sausage, cabbage soup with ham, or chickpea and spicy sausage —in fact, any soup that uses pork. It's also perfect for making white sauce to go with boiled ham—and, naturally, forms the ideal base for the gravy to pour over roast pork. The addition of cloves and allspice in this recipe helps the digestion of the slightly higher fat content of pork and its related products.

about 2lb ham bones

2 large red onions, coarsely chopped

2 large carrots, coarsely chopped

1 large leek, coarsely chopped

2 large celery sticks, chopped

6 cloves

1 teaspoon allspice

5 bay leaves

10 black peppercorns

2 quarts water

½ teaspoon salt

Put all the ingredients into a large saucepan.

Bring to a boil and simmer slowly for about 4 hours, skimming regularly with a slotted spoon to remove the fat.

Strain through kitchen cheesecloth or a strainer.

Leave, covered, until completely cold.

Skim off any solidified fat.

the proper stuff: with great flavor and no commercial additives

beef stock

The true flavor of beef stock is the most difficult of all to reproduce as a bouillon cube without the addition of chemical additives, especially the awful monosodium glutamate. The delicate and unique taste of homemade beef stock is one of the most glorious delights of the kitchen, as well as being the cheapest—your butcher will normally give you the bones for nothing when you buy other meat or poultry.

about 2lb meat bones, sawn into 1½-inch pieces by your butcher

2 large red onions, coarsely chopped

2 large carrots, coarsely chopped

1 large leek, coarsely chopped

2 large celery sticks, chopped

1 large bunch of sage

1 sprig of rosemary

5 bay leaves

10 black peppercorns

2 quarts water

½ teaspoon salt

Roast the meat bones for about 30 minutes at 450°F.

Put them and any scrapings into a large saucepan.

Add the rest of the ingredients.

Bring to a boil and simmer slowly for about 4 hours, skimming regularly with a slotted spoon to remove the fat.

Strain through kitchen cheesecloth or a strainer.

Leave, covered, until completely cold.

Skim off any solidified fat.

immune-
boosting
soups

introduction 20
creamy watercress soup 22
white onion soup 23
chinese bok-choy and chicken soup 24
bread and garlic soup 26
welsh minestrone with rice and leeks 27
cabbage soup with ham 28
chicken, chile, chard, and noodle soup 30
duck soup with prunes 31

For generations, the wonderful healers who have inhabited kitchens throughout the world have known about the health-boosting properties of soup. Made properly, soup contains some of the most powerful ingredients that can be used in what is often referred to as "kitchen medicine."

Unfortunately, however (and detrimentally to us all), within the rarefied, scientific atmosphere of late 20th-century Western medical practice, the whole idea of food as medicine became viewed as backward, superstitious, or even downright ridiculous.

Happily, 21st-century medicine has a taken a much more enlightened approach to the subject. Today, a growing body of scientific evidence backs up the ancient idea that "we are what we eat." Many scientific studies have shown that common foods do indeed have the ability to kill off harmful bacteria and fungal infections. Phytochemicals—natural substances that occur in plants—exert a wide range of beneficial actions on the body, some of them concerned specifically with boosting natural immunity.

In our modern world, the body's immune system is under constant attack from pollutants, pesticides, herbicides, fungicides, and all the chemical detritus of so-called civilization. For this reason, it is even more important that highly protective antioxidant nutrients feature as widely as possible in day-to-day meals—which is precisely why the following recipes were included in this book. All the soups in this chapter can directly improve and boost your body's natural defenses to infection and damage, so it is vital to have them on a regular basis. When there's an epidemic of flu, colds, or chest infections, use them more often to ensure that you escape whichever bug is doing the rounds. Even if you have picked up an infection, immune-boosting soups are still essential eating, as they help shorten the duration of your illness.

The soups in this chapter rely heavily on the foods richest in the natural chemicals that help the body protect itself by safeguarding its cells. Cabbage, for example, is full of cancer-fighting phytochemicals as well as natural sulfur, which is antibacterial. Onions, garlic, and leeks contain powerful sulfurous allicins—substances that attack bacteria, viruses, and fungi. Poultry, such as chicken and duck, contains enzymes and B vitamins that enhance immunity. And all the bright green, yellow, and orange vegetables are a major source of carotenoids—natural pigments that play an important role in good health.

When reading this chapter, don't be put off by seemingly strange combinations or unfamiliar foods in some of the recipes. You might think, for instance, that prunes are an odd ingredient to include in a soup (*see* Duck soup with prunes, page 31), but in fact they are one of nature's richest sources of antioxidants. Few people get enough of these powerful immune-boosting substances, yet we all need them in abundance as part of our constant fight against infection, disease, and illness.

Most of the herbs and spices in the recipes are included for their flavor, but they play health-giving roles as well. Bay leaves, thyme, rosemary, chilies, and oregano are all rich in volatile essential oils, substances that stimulate immune activity. This means that the blood's protective white cells are encouraged to attack and destroy invading organisms.

For all their scientific-sounding benefits, immune-boosting soups take us back to the roots of peasant cooking: they're easy to prepare, inexpensive to make, and simply bursting with flavor, nutrients, and everything you need for bodily self-defense. This is the true essence of kitchen medicine—something most people today consider merits much more than ridicule.

creamy watercress soup

In addition to having a wonderful peppery flavor, watercress is one of the most important immune-protectors you can eat. If you are a smoker, eat this soup twice a week, as it may well reduce your chances of lung cancer. There's an additional benefit from the protective probiotic bacteria in live yogurt. It is well known that these "good bugs" are not only part of the body's natural defenses, but they also release specific chemicals that enhance the effectiveness of the immune system.

7 tablespoons unsalted butter

4 large scallions, finely sliced

1 large bunch or bag of watercress—about 12oz

4 cups Vegetable Stock (*see* page 13)

bouquet garni: 3 sprigs each parsley, thyme, and rosemary, tied together with string, or a good commercial bouquet garni bag

¾ cup plain probiotic yogurt

In a large pan, melt the butter, then gently sweat the scallions for 3 minutes.

Pull the leaves off any thick watercress stems; discard the thicker stems.

Add the watercress to the pan and stir briskly for 1 minute.

Add the stock and bouquet garni.

Simmer for 10 minutes, then remove the bouquet garni.

Blend until smooth and return to the pan.

Add the yogurt and stir thoroughly.

Serve hot with Herb croutons (*see* page 128). Alternatively, serve cold as a delicious summer soup.

to protect the lungs ...
Watercress contains **antibacterial** mustard oils, lots of **betacarotene**, and a **phytochemical** that protects the cells of lung tissue against the carcinogenic effects of smoking

white onion soup

Onions have a long tradition in folk medicine, particularly for helping the body overcome the effects of chest infections. In this recipe, this healing property is combined with the protective essential oils from bay leaves, thyme and rosemary to make a delicious and health-giving, flavor-packed soup.

4 tablespoons unsalted butter

1lb 2oz white Spanish onions, very finely sliced

3 tablespoons flour

4 cups whole milk

4 bay leaves

10 peppercorns, slightly crushed

bouquet garni: 3 sprigs each parsley, thyme, and rosemary, tied together with string, or a good commercial bouquet garni bag

1 bunch of flat leaf parsley, finely chopped

Melt the butter over very low heat.

Add the onions. Stir until thoroughly coated, then cover and allow to sweat gently for 10 minutes.

Sift in the flour and cook for another 5 minutes, stirring continuously.

Pour in the milk and add the bay leaves, peppercorns, and bouquet garni.

Simmer very gently for about 10 minutes, until the onions are quite soft.

Remove the bay leaves and bouquet garni, and strain out the peppercorns.

Serve garnished generously with chopped parsley and Rouille (*see* page 129) or Potato floaters (*see* page 131).

for fighting chest infections ...
Onions offer **antiviral** and **antibacterial** protection
Parsley, a **diuretic**, aids the natural cleansing process

chinese bok choy and chicken soup

Bok choy is another member of the cabbage family that offers good all-round protection from germs. The good news is that this tasty vegetable is now widely available and is easy to prepare. When combined with immune-boosting scallions, garlic, and chicken stock, it creates a power-packed super soup that provides a real boost to your system.

6 large scallions

¼ cup canola oil

2 garlic cloves, peeled and crushed

5 cups Chicken Stock (*see* page 15)

2 chicken breasts, skinned and finely shredded along the grain of the flesh

4 heads of bok choy, thick stems reserved, leaves finely chopped

5½oz Chinese noodles or vermicelli (optional)

1 teaspoon light soy sauce

Very finely chop the white parts of 4 of the scallions; cut the others lengthwise almost to the root and reserve.

Heat the oil very gently. Add the chopped scallions and garlic and sweat for just 2 minutes.

Pour in the stock. Bring slowly to a simmer.

Add the chicken and reserved bok choy stems, and simmer for 10 minutes, until the chicken is almost tender.

Remove the bok choy stems.

Add the bok choy leaves, noodles (if using), and soy sauce and simmer for 5 minutes.

Serve with the reserved scallions and Rice fritters (*see* page 130) floating on top.

to strengthen the immune system ...
Bok choy contains protective **thiocyanates**, and large amounts of **betacarotene** for good cell health

bread and garlic soup

There are many variations of this soup throughout Spain, and to judge from the number I've tried, every family must have its own favorite recipe. This is mine. If garlic's potency puts you off, take heart: cooking it this way seems to prevent the residual garlic breath, so be brave and give it a try if you want a bowlful of super-immunity.

5 tablespoons olive oil

1 head of garlic, split into cloves, finely chopped

4 thick slices of whole-wheat bread (crusts removed), made into bread crumbs

6 cups Vegetable Stock (*see* page 13)

small handful of fresh oregano or 2 generous pinches of the dried herb

4 eggs

Heat the oil gently in a large pan.

Add the chopped garlic, cover, and sweat slowly for 3 minutes.

Tip in the bread crumbs, vegetable stock, and oregano.

Keep covered and simmer for 2 minutes, adding more stock if the mixture gets too thick.

Beat the eggs. Add to the pan and simmer very gently for 2 more minutes.

Serve with Herb croutons (*see* page 128).

to help fight bacteria …
Garlic contains powerful **antibacterial substances**
Oregano adds antiseptic **thymol**
Eggs provide health-giving **B vitamins**

welsh minestrone
with rice and leeks

The Roman emperor Nero used to eat leeks every day to protect his voice. It's no wonder that this vegetable is the national emblem of Wales, a nation renowned for its singing. When coughs, cold, flu, and sore throats abound, nothing could be better than this wonderfully thick cornucopia of germ-fighting nutrients. What's more, it tastes terrific.

3 tablespoons extra virgin olive oil

3 Welsh onions (or 1 ordinary onion), chopped

2 leeks, finely sliced

2 cups mixed root vegetables, finely diced

5 cups Vegetable Stock (*see* page 13)

½ cup long-grain rice

⅔ cup peas, fresh or frozen

1 cup green beans, cut into ¾-inch slices

Heat the olive oil and gently sweat the onions and leeks for 5 minutes.

Add the diced vegetables. Stir until thoroughly coated with oil.

Pour in the stock and rice and simmer for 15 minutes.

Add the peas and beans and continue simmering until tender.

for protection against colds and flu ...
Root vegetables offer a **mineral boost**
Beans and peas provide natural **plant hormones**
Leeks add protective **phytochemicals**

immune-boosting soups   27

cabbage soup with ham

Cabbage has been the medicine of the poor since a pot was first hung over a fire in prehistoric times. Of all the vegetables, cabbage and its relatives must be regarded as among the most important for their medicinal value. This soup also provides a good dose of protein from the ham, and immune-enhancing carotenoids from the vegetable stock.

10½oz ham (or more for a very robust soup), fat removed

¼ cup extra virgin olive oil

2 red onions, finely chopped

6 cups Vegetable Stock (*see* page 13)

2 cups cubed potatoes

1lb 2oz Savoy cabbage, finely shredded

7oz noodles or spaghettini

Cube the ham, dry-fry until browned and reserve.

Heat the oil.

Add the onions and sweat for 5 minutes in the oil.

Add the stock and the potatoes and simmer until the potatoes are just tender.

Blend in a food processor or blender until smooth.

Return to the pan and bring back to a simmer.

Add the cabbage and cook for 5 minutes.

Stir in the noodles and the ham and continue cooking for about 3–4 minutes until the noodles are al dente.

Serve with Beet floaters (*see* page 131).

for prevention and protection ...
Cabbage is rich in **antibacterial sulfur**
and cancer-fighting **thiocynates**
Potatoes provide **vitamin C**

chicken, chile, chard, and noodle soup

You'll obtain plenty of health benefits here from the traditional immune-strengthening properties of chicken soup. In addition to the health-promoting benefits of chard and chile, the egg noodles provide a little iron and easily absorbed energy—always important in the body's fight against infection.

3 tablespoons extra virgin olive oil

1 large onion, very finely chopped

1 red chile, seeds removed, very finely chopped

5 cups Chicken Stock (*see* page 15)

5½oz chard, stems torn from the leaves

9oz egg noodles

Heat the olive oil and sweat the onion and chile gently for 5 minutes.

Add the stock, bring to a boil, then simmer for 10 minutes.

Strain into a clean saucepan.

Slice the chard stems very finely, add to the pan and simmer for 10 minutes.

Tear the chard leaves coarsely and add to the pan along with the noodles.

Simmer until tender—usually not more than 3 minutes.

to aid in the fight against infection ...
Chard is an amazing source of **betacarotenes**
Chilies contain **capsaicin**, which stimulates the circulation

duck soup with prunes

Duck, like chicken, is a delicious source of a whole host of vitamins and minerals. The unusual addition of prunes makes this soup an extremely high source of protective antioxidants, and their slight sweetness is balanced by the parsley, thyme, and rosemary, which also provide beneficial essential oils.

1 cooked duck carcass, some flesh still attached, but with all the skin and visible fat removed

2 bay leaves

bouquet garni: 3 sprigs each parsley, thyme, and rosemary, tied together with string, or a good commercial bouquet garni bag

1 large onion, finely chopped

2 large carrots, coarsely chopped

2 celery sticks, coarsely chopped

10 peppercorns

up to 6 cups Vegetable Stock (*see* page 13)

1 cup pitted prunes (or dried apricots, if preferred)

Put all the ingredients except the prunes into a large saucepan.

Bring to a boil and simmer for 1 hour.

Strain into a bowl.

Set aside the duck. Discard the bouquet garni and push some of the vegetables through a strainer into the stock, depending on how thick you would like the soup. Add enough stock to give the quantity and texture you prefer.

When the duck is cool enough to handle, scrape off any remaining meat and add to the stock.

Chop or snip the prunes into peanut-size pieces.

Add to the pan and simmer gently for 20 minutes.

to fortify general immunity ...
Duck is rich in body-building **protein**, protective **enzymes**, and **B vitamins**
Bay leaves provide **cineole** and **laurenolide**, essential oils that fight respiratory infections

circulation soups

introduction 34
spiced lentil soup 36
curried parsnip and vegetable soup 38
ginger, leek, and carrot soup 39
beet soup 41
oat and broccoli soup 42
oxtail soup 43
sweet cherry soup 44

Soups are often associated with the chilly, damp, dark, and depressing days of winter, when a steaming bowl of hot broth brings much-needed warmth to icy hands and feet. In fact, the physical effect of soup has far more to do with its ingredients than with the temperature of the soup itself.

Naturally, there is a powerful psychological benefit to be gained from cupping your hands around a steaming bowl of hot goodness, but this can't be relied upon to set the blood coursing through your veins. Many people need a circulation boost in all weathers, not just in winter. While the capillaries—the tiniest blood vessels at the very end of the circulatory system—naturally constrict in cold weather to conserve body heat, people who suffer from poor circulation endure cool extremities all year round. The problem is more common in women than men, even when the former are in otherwise perfect health.

As irritating as these milder cases are, those who have an illness called Raynaud's disease have more severe circulatory problems. This condition shuts down the blood supply to the outer parts of the body; although it most commonly affects the hands and fingers, it can also occur in the feet, toes, nose, and even the ears. What triggers the onset of Raynaud's is hard to predict. Simple factors, such as stepping into an air-conditioned room on a hot summer's day, can cause the fingers to go parchment white and become "dead-feeling" and painful. Eventually, they may turn blue or black, and when the blood finally begins to flow again, the pain becomes even more unbearable. Fortunately, help is on hand.

Whether it's cold weather, poor circulation, Raynaud's disease, or any other circulatory problem, the circulation soups in this chapter will come to the rescue. Just as in the previous chapter, the recipes here employ the benefits of onions, leeks, and garlic, all of which help improve blood-flow. Then there are the advantages of beets, used for centuries in eastern Europe as a traditional remedy to improve the quality of blood and its circulation. Special emphasis is also given to a group of nutrients called bioflavonoids, which are vital for maintaining the health and integrity of blood-vessel walls. One of the richest sources of these natural protectors is cherries. And yes, you can make soup from cherries—just *see* page 44.

Spices are renowned for the dramatic way in which they stimulate the circulation; who hasn't broken into a sweat, for example, halfway through a bowl of curry or chile con carne? Ginger, curry mixtures, chiles, horseradish, mustard seeds, and all other hot spices are used in these recipes to help improve the way blood moves around the body.

Two factors that can severely affect circulation are the clotting tendency of blood and high levels of cholesterol. Cholesterol is deposited on the inside of the artery walls, which results in the narrowing of these vessels, making it more difficult for the blood to get through. Major ingredients that specifically target both these problems are the monounsaturated fats in olive oil, natural phytochemicals in garlic, onions, and leeks, and the soluble fiber in oats, lentils and root vegetables. All of these work to eliminate cholesterol from the body and lower the risk of fatty deposits in the arteries, as well as reducing the stickiness of the blood so that it flows more easily.

Winter or summer, the benefits of these delicious soups will help maintain the efficiency and effectiveness of your body's circulation. The bonus is that they're all also extremely rich in the vital nutrients that contribute to your general health—protecting you against many other diseases at the same time.

spiced lentil soup

In this soup, spices come into their own, working together to get your circulation buzzing. Add B vitamins and good fiber from the lentils, plus calcium, phosphorus, and magnesium from the coconut milk, and you have an effective, delicious, and satisfying dish for circulatory health.

3 tablespoons extra virgin olive oil

1 onion, finely sliced

1 garlic clove, finely chopped

1 inch fresh ginger root, peeled and finely grated

1 tablespoon coriander seed, well crushed

1 tablespoon allspice

1 teaspoon chili powder

3 cups Vegetable Stock (*see* page 13)

1²⁄₃ cups canned coconut milk

¾ cup green lentils

Heat the olive oil in a large saucepan.

Stir in the onion and sweat gently for 5 minutes.

Add the garlic and ginger and continue sweating for 4 minutes.

Stir in the coriander, allspice, and chili powder and cook, stirring continuously, for 3 minutes.

Add the stock and coconut milk and bring to a simmer.

Stir in the lentils and continue to simmer for about 30 minutes.

to spice up your blood-flow ...
Ginger provides **gingeroles**, essential oils that dilate blood vessels
Chile adds **capsaicin** for stimulating warmth

curried parsnip and vegetable soup

Putting parsnips together with stimulating spices, such as those in curry powder, produces a soup that is seriously good for your circulation. Adding beans and peas increases the fiber content and supplies beneficial protein, while the crème fraîche gives it a wonderfully creamy texture and supplies calcium, too.

¼ cup extra virgin olive oil

1 large onion, finely chopped

1 heaping tablespoon curry powder

2 tablespoons flour

2 parsnips (about 1lb 2oz in total), diced

5 cups Vegetable Stock (*see* page 13)

¾ cup crème fraîche or sour cream

1 cup green beans, cut into 1-inch fingers

⅔ cup peas, fresh or frozen

Heat the olive oil and gently sweat the onions for 10 minutes.

Remove from the heat and stir in the curry powder and flour.

Return to the heat and cook, stirring continuously, for 3 minutes.

Add the diced parsnips and stir for 2 more minutes.

Pour in the stock and bring to a boil.

Simmer for 20 minutes or until the parsnips are tender.

Blend the mixture, return to the pan, and bring back to a simmer.

Stir in the crème fraîche.

Add the beans and peas and cook for another 7 minutes.

to keep blood flowing freely ...
Parsnips are rich in **minerals** and **fiber**
Beans and peas supply beneficial **plant hormones**

ginger, leek, and carrot soup

The leek is a member of the *Allium* genus of plants and, just like its onion and garlic relatives, it is a rich source of natural sulfur-based chemicals that improve the circulation. This recipe provides a triple boost from all three. As an extra circulatory bonus, there's plenty of ginger as well.

1 tablespoons extra virgin olive oil

1 large red onion, finely sliced

3 plump garlic cloves, finely chopped

3 large leeks, finely chopped

1 inch fresh ginger root, peeled and grated

2¼lb carrots, finely diced

5 cups Vegetable Stock (*see* page 13)

Heat the olive oil in a large saucepan.

Add the onion, garlic, leeks, and ginger and sweat gently for 10 minutes.

Drop in the carrot cubes and stir until covered with the oil mixture.

Pour in the stock and bring to a boil.

Turn down the heat and simmer until the carrots are tender—about 20 minutes.

Blend in a food processor or blender.

Pour through a fine sieve, being careful to remove any stringy ginger.

Note: this soup is delicious hot or cold. If you're in a rush, use carrot or vegetable juice instead of fresh carrots. You could also combine orange with carrot juice and use store-bought crushed ginger. This puts up the price, but remember, this recipe makes enough to last 2 or 3 days.

for reducing blood pressure ...
Leeks contain **phytochemicals** that help lower cholesterol, which keeps blood-pressure levels down

beet soup

Throughout eastern Europe, beet is renowned for its blood- and circulation-boosting properties. Served as soup or juice, this vegetable has been used in the treatment of anemia, poor circulation, and even leukemia. In this recipe, it is combined with carrots and lemon juice to provide a refreshing, nourishing soup for healthy blood.

2¼lb fresh, raw beets (pickled ones are not suitable)

2 large carrots

1 garlic clove, peeled

1 onion, peeled

5 tablespoons extra virgin olive oil

6 cups Vegetable Stock (*see* page 13)

juice of 1 lemon

1⅔ cups plain yogurt

Shred the beets, carrots, garlic, and onion, or chop them in a food processor.

Heat the oil in a large saucepan. Add the vegetables and sweat gently for 10 minutes.

Add the stock and simmer, covered, for 40 minutes.

Strain into a clean saucepan and bring back to a simmer.

Stir the lemon juice into the yogurt.

Serve the soup with a swirl of the lemon yogurt on top and Beet floaters (*see* page 131).

Alternatively, serve cold, substituting white seedless grapes for the lemon yogurt.

for a traditional circulation treatment …

Beets are rich in **iron**, which helps prevent anemia
Carrots supply **betacarotene** to protect capillaries
Vitamin C in lemons prevents damage to artery walls

oat and broccoli soup

As well as being a healthy breakfast food in the form of oatmeal, oats are a versatile ingredient and can be used to delicious advantage in many other ways. In this unusual soup, they're combined with broccoli to make a surprisingly light and delicate dish that offers huge health benefits.

2 tablespoons extra virgin olive oil

6 scallions, finely chopped

1lb 5oz broccoli florets, halved if very large

½ cup steel-cut oats

3 cups lowfat milk

750ml (27fl oz) Vegetable Stock (*see* page 13)

sea salt and black pepper

¼ plain yogurt

generous bunch of chives, finely snipped

Heat the oil gently, then sweat the scallions until soft—about 5 minutes.

Add the broccoli and continue heating gently, stirring continuously, for 3 more minutes.

Mix in the oats and continue cooking for 4 minutes, still stirring.

Pour in the milk and stock, cover and simmer for 10 minutes; season with salt and pepper to taste.

Serve with a spoonful of yogurt in each bowl.

Sprinkle with the chives or with Herb croutons (*see* page 128).

Note: top each dish with a chive flower for a more sophisticated look.

to protect the heart …
Oats are rich in **B vitamins** and **soluble fiber**
Broccoli supplies **vitamin C** and **betacarotene**, which protect the heart and can help to prevent cancer

oxtail soup

I can't recommend this robust, hearty soup strongly enough. With the stimulating spices in Worcestershire or Tabasco sauce, it is sure to warm the cockles of your heart.

about 8 × 1-inch chunks of oxtail

1 cup flour, seasoned with plenty of black pepper and a little sea salt

5 tablespoons extra virgin olive oil

1 large onion, coarsely chopped

2 garlic cloves, peeled and finely chopped

1 large carrot, very finely diced

1 turnip, finely diced

½ large rutabaga, finely diced

6 cups Beef Stock (*see* page 17)

3 tablespoons tomato paste

2 teaspoons Worcestershire or Tabasco sauce

2 bay leaves

1 generous handful of parsley, finely chopped

Trim as much fat as possible off the oxtail.

Coat the meat in the seasoned flour and set aside.

In a large saucepan, heat the olive oil and gently sweat the vegetables for 10 minutes, stirring continuously.

In another pan, sear the floured oxtail in a little more oil.

Add the meat to the vegetable pan.

Pour in the stock and add the tomato paste, Worcestershire sauce, and bay leaves.

Cover and simmer gently for 50 minutes, or until the meat is tender.

Remove the bay leaves.

Serve the oxtail on or off the bone and sprinkled with the parsley.

Note: for a more sustaining main meal, add baby potatoes just as the soup comes to a simmer.

to revitalize the circulatory system ...
Oxtail is bursting with **B vitamins** and **iron** for healthy blood
Turnip, rutabaga, and carrot provide **betacarotene**
and **minerals** for good circulation

sweet cherry soup

It's easy to think of cherries as simply one of those delicious summer treats, but they're much more than that. Ripe, plump cherries are a storehouse of circulation-boosting nutrients. Combined with an extra dose of vitamin C from the cranberry juice, this soup will benefit anyone's circulatory system.

2¼lb cherries, pitted weight

1 cup cranberry juice

2 cups water

½ cup glass sweet white wine, such as Muscat de Beaumes de Venise or Monbazillac

1 tablespoon arrowroot

4 sprigs of mint

Process the cherries in a food processor or blender, then strain to remove the skins.

Put the pulp into a large pan with the cranberry juice, water, and wine and bring slowly to a boil, stirring well.

Stir the arrowroot into 2 more tablespoons of water and mix thoroughly.

Pour the arrowroot mixture into the fruit stock and stir continuously until slightly thickened.

Serve garnished with the sprigs of mint.

Note: this soup is delicious warm or cold. You can make it with other summer fruits, particularly strawberries, and replace the wine with extra fruit juice if you're serving children.

for a circulatory boost ...
Cherries are rich in **bioflavonoids** and **vitamin C**, both of which support healthy blood

skin-reviving soups

introduction 48

iced fennel soup 50

carrot and almond cream 51

sweet potato and garlic soup 52

spicy carrot and orange soup 54

corn and smoked haddock chowder 55

pumpkin soup with nasturtium flowers 56

The eyes may be the mirrors of the soul, but as many modern doctors now admit, your skin is an accurate mirror of your eating habits. Of course, no food or special diet is a cure for every skin condition.

But no matter what problem you're having, the food you eat can help it to improve, or conversely, can aggravate things so much that even a minor skin disorder rapidly degenerates into a catastrophe—which can plunge you into despair, especially if you're an already image-conscious teenager. For some sufferers, the psychological ramifications of acne, eczema, and psoriasis can be so profound that they radically alter their personality. For both men and women, any condition perceived as being embarrassing, disfiguring, or abnormal can lead to withdrawal from social activities, isolation, lack of achievement at school, college, or work—and possibly even clinical depression.

This triggers an inevitable vicious circle: "My acne is bad, I'm unattractive; I'm embarrassed; I won't go out with my friends; I'm ugly; I don't have any friends; I'm miserable; I deserve three doughnuts, a slab of chocolate, and a bottle of wine; I wake up feeling sick; I've got a hangover; my acne is worse; I'm more depressed; I'll have more chocolate and wine..."

Okay, so this is an extreme scenario, but believe me, it does happen. I've seen it in so many of my patients. It doesn't matter what age you are or the circumstances in which you live, any skin problem can be a disaster. This is one situation in which molehills often turn into mountains. The spot on your nose on the day of an important interview or your first date suddenly seems the size of a golf ball. That patch of gray, flaky eczema under your eyes is bound to flare up the day before your wedding. And halfway through the meal with your prospective in-laws, you just know that you'll come out in hives. That's why this chapter on skin-reviving soups has been included: to take the strain out of such "personal appearances." Not only do these soups help you over the hurdles as they appear, but by including these recipes regularly in your normal weekly eating plan, you'll be doing everything you can to nourish, heal, protect, and revitalize your skin.

If you really want to keep those zits at bay, my advice is to eat soup. It's certainly a cheaper (and healthier) option than covering yourself with expensive facial products, many of which do nothing more than moisturize the skin. The most important of the skin nutrients abound in some of the most inexpensive, simple, and easy-to-cook foods. Betacarotene, for example, is a major ingredient in carrots, pumpkins, sweet potatoes, and corn, none of which will make a dent in your budget. Yet this nutrient is one of the best friends your skin has. The stuff that gives these vegetables their colour also functions as a protective antioxidant, meaning it's anti-aging as well.

What's more, all root vegetables are rich in minerals, particularly skin-friendly zinc. The vitamin C from oranges, potatoes, and leeks is also essential for natural resistance to a wide range of infections. In addition, the sulfur compounds present in onions, leeks, chives, scallions, and garlic are powerful weapons in your skin's fight against bacterial and fungal infections. When it comes to conditions such as dry skin, eczema, and psoriasis, the healing effects of vitamin E—found in olive oil, almonds, and egg yolks—are second to none. Finally, the natural anti-inflammatory properties of the essential oil known as gingerol, found in fresh ginger, can help take the sting out of most skin disorders.

Of course, these soups are good for more than giving your skin the vital bloom and glowing texture it deserves. Like most recipes in this book, these skin-reviving soups all look good, taste great, and will help the rest of your body feel good into the bargain.

iced fennel soup

The familiar, subtle, and delicate taste of Florence fennel comes from its high content of essential oils. These can help reduce the amount of a fatty substance known as sebum, which is excreted by the skin; that reduction, in turn, helps prevent acne.

2 large bulbs of Florence fennel, roughly chopped, fronds reserved

1lb 2oz small new potatoes, unpeeled

4 cups Vegetable Stock (*see* page 13)

2 cloves

1¼ cups milk

½ teaspoon grated nutmeg

Put the chopped fennel and potatoes in a large saucepan with the stock and cloves. Simmer for 20 minutes.

Remove from the heat and discard the cloves.

Blend the mixture, then return to the heat and add the milk.

Transfer to a large bowl and, when cool enough, cover and put into the fridge.

In the meantime, chop the reserved fennel fronds and sprinkle them into an ice-cube tray. Fill with water and freeze.

Serve the soup with a couple of ice cubes in each dish and a sprinkle of nutmeg on top.

to soothe irritated skin ...
Fennel bulbs are rich in **fenchone**, a gentle liver stimulant that improves the breakdown, digestion, and elimination of dietary fats

carrot and almond cream

Using carrots to combat skin problems shouldn't be a surprise. Of all the root vegetables, they're the best to help with any skin disorder, owing to their high content of healing phytochemicals. Almonds give this soup a hefty boost of minerals, while leeks provide antibacterial sulfur compounds, and egg yolks are a rich source of iron and vitamin E—both vital for supple, smooth skin.

3 tablespoons extra virgin olive oil

1 large leek, finely sliced

5 cups Vegetable Stock (*see* page 13)

4 large carrots, sliced

1 cup ground almonds

1 cup heavy cream

2 egg yolks

In a large saucepan, heat the oil and sweat the leek gently for about 5 minutes.

Add the stock, carrots, and ground almonds and simmer until the vegetables are tender—around 10–15 minutes.

Whisk together the cream and egg yolks.

Blend the carrot and almond mixture. Pour into the cream and egg yolks, whisking or stirring thoroughly.

Reheat gently.

For a very finely textured soup, push the mixture through a strainer, or strain through kitchen cheesecloth (I never bother).

Serve with Emmental croutons (*see* page 128).

for skin nourishment and health ...
Carrots are packed with **betacarotene**, essential for healthy skin
Almonds supply **zinc** and **selenium** to nourish the skin

sweet potato and garlic soup

Also sometimes known as a "yam", the sweet potato is one of the nicest and healthiest introductions from the tropical regions of the Americas and, thanks to its massive content of betacarotene, is great skin food however you eat it.

2 heads of garlic

1lb 10oz sweet potatoes, cubed

6 cups Vegetable Stock (*see* page 13)

Cut the tops off the heads of garlic, but don't peel them. Wrap in foil and roast at 400°F for 15–20 minutes, depending on size.

Meanwhile, simmer the sweet potatoes in the stock and blend until smooth using a food processor or blender.

Cool the garlic until it's comfortable to handle, then squeeze out the pulp.

Put the sweet potato mixture back on the heat. Add the garlic pulp and whisk thoroughly.

Serve garnished with Onion floaters (*see* page 131).

to prevent dry skin and infection ...
Sweet potatoes provide vital **betacarotene** and **vitamin E** to help dry, fragile skin
Garlic helps prevent fungal infections and acne

spicy carrot and orange soup

This quick and easy soup is very inexpensive, full of nutrients, and looks spectacular served in white bowls as an appetizer for a dinner party. Its powerhouse of healing skin essentials and terrific taste make it ideal in winter or summer, so serve it all year round to revitalize your complexion.

¼ cup extra virgin olive oil

1 large onion, finely chopped

1 inch fresh root ginger, peeled and grated

2lb carrots, sliced

6 cups water

2 cups fresh orange juice

¼ cup light cream

Heat the oil in a large saucepan, then sweat the onion and ginger gently until soft.

Add the carrots to the pan and coat with the oil.

Pour in the water and orange juice and simmer until the carrots are tender—usually 10–15 minutes, depending on how finely they're sliced.

Process or blend until smooth.

Pour into bowls and serve with swirls of cream on top.

for a good dose of skin protection …
Olive oil is rich in essential **vitamin E**
Carrots supply vital **betacarotene**
Orange juice provides immune-boosting **vitamin C**

corn and smoked haddock chowder

The Scottish tradition of making soup from smoked haddock is centuries old. Haddock is a rich source of perfect protein without saturated fat, and it also supplies significant amounts of essential minerals. What's more, when combined with corn and healing herbs, it makes a hearty, healthy chowder.

1lb 5oz undyed, naturally smoked haddock, skinned and boned

4 cups milk

4 bay leaves

2 sprigs each of parsley, dill, sage, and thyme, tied together with string

6 scallions, finely sliced

1 cup Fish Stock (*see* page 14)

2 cups corn kernels preferably fresh from the ear, but canned or frozen will do

½ cup light cream

Put the smoked haddock and milk into a pan.

Add the bay leaves, herbs, and scallions.

Simmer for 10 minutes and allow to cool.

Remove the bay leaves and herbs.

Strain the fish from the milk, reserving both.

Put the stock and the milk into a large pan.

Add the corn kernels and simmer for 5 minutes.

Flake the fish and add to the pan along with the cream.

Serve warm with a spoonful of Rouille (*see* page 129) or Herb croutons (*see* page 128) on top.

to cleanse the skin ...
Haddock is rich in **iodine**, which helps regulate the thyroid gland
Corn provides essential **vitamin A**
Sage and thyme offer cleansing, **antiseptic essential oils**

skin-reviving soups 55

pumpkin soup with nasturtium flowers

How sad that pumpkins, with their wonderful flavor and nutritional value, only tend to be bought for Halloween—and even then, they're wasted as decorative jack-o'-lanterns. Yet pumpkins are perfect as a healthy alternative to stodgier winter foods, and in this soup they help counteract the dehydrating effects of central heating. Topped with nasturtium flowers, this is one dish that looks as delicious as it tastes.

2 large, white onions, finely chopped

2 garlic cloves, finely chopped

2 tablespoons extra virgin olive oil

2 tablespoons unsalted butter

1 tablespoon curry powder or paste

4 cups Vegetable Stock (*see* page 13)

1¼lb pumpkin (or summer squash or zucchini) deseeded and cubed

¼ cup crème fraîche or sour cream

4 nasturtium flowers (if unavailable, use chive flowers)

Sweat the onions and garlic gently in the oil and butter.

Add the curry powder and cook for 2 minutes, stirring continuously.

Pour in the vegetable stock and bring to a boil.

Add the pumpkin to the stock.

Simmer until the vegetables are just tender.

Blend in a food processor or blender.

Stir in the crème fraîche and mix thoroughly.

Serve with nasturtium flowers or Zucchini floaters (*see* page 131) on top.

to lift and rejuvenate the complexion …
Pumpkin gives a boost of **betacarotene** and **folic acid**
Nasturtium flowers are rich in **antibacterial mustard oils**

sexy soups

introduction 60
vegetable broth with poached egg 62
chilled yogurt and cucumber soup 64
lettuce, mint, and pea soup 65
thai sweet-and-sour soup 66
asparagus soup 68
game soup 69
mussel chowder 71

It's extraordinary that with increasing media focus on sex, there appears to be a directly proportional growth in sexual problems. As strange as it seems, the more people see of it in the movies, on television, and in print, the less they seem able to "perform" in their own bedrooms.

While it's true that some sexual problems have a psychological root, the percentage of people, both men and women, whose physical relationships are less than satisfactory is now known to be far greater than was previously thought. Male impotence, loss of libido in both sexes, fertility problems, and a marked decline in women's arousal and satisfaction are all problems faced by many otherwise happy and compatible couples.

From a medical point of view, it is known that a range of underlying conditions can affect sexual performance and enjoyment. High blood pressure, raised cholesterol levels, diabetes, heart disease, circulatory difficulties, neurological disorders, and even simple diseases of wear and tear, such as osteoarthritis, can all interfere with the ability to perform or enjoy everyday sexual relationships. To make matters worse, the medication prescribed for some of these conditions can also have a devastating effect on libido and erectile function.

But the trouble doesn't stop there. The single largest factor in this equation is food: specifically, a regular, long-term intake of food that supplies only marginal amounts of some of the key sexually essential ingredients. Over 50 percent of women attending fertility clinics have been on some form of drastic weight-loss diet in the 12 months prior to their visit. Sperm counts in men have halved in the last three decades. This rise in sexual problems has gone hand in hand with a decreasing nutritional content in food caused by intensive farming, and with pollution by insecticides, pesticides, and hormone-disrupting chemicals. It has been compounded by a rising consumption of high-fat, high-salt, and high-sugar foods.

Scientists may poke fun at the idea of aphrodisiac foods, but many ingredients in the following recipes have been used for centuries as sexual stimulants. The fact is that nutrients such as zinc, selenium, iron, iodine, and vitamins A, C, and E all play a well-researched part in the ability to achieve and maintain satisfaction through successful sexual activity. Worryingly, these are the very nutrients that have declined most in the average Western diet.

That is why they are used liberally in "Sexy Soups." The recipes in this chapter aren't just designed to give your sex life a boost; they've been created to taste good, look appealing, and provide the sensations of sensuality that are essential for loving sexuality. Shrimp, for example, are rich in zinc: vital for sperm formation. When married with the heady aroma of lemon grass and the circulatory booster of cilantro, they create a stimulating sweet-and-sour soup (*see* page 66). Given their vitamin E and iron content, it is no coincidence that eggs are a universal symbol of fertility; they're featured on page 62. The combination of yogurt, mint, and garlic has a long aphrodisiacal tradition in folklore. It is used on page 64 in a fabulous chilled soup that sets the scene for a night of consuming passion.

Although traditionally thought to be a great male aphrodisiac because of their extremely high zinc content, mollusks contain essential fatty acids that can have the same effect on women. One large bowl of Mussel chowder (*see* page 71) shared intimately between lovers is all you need. Equally dramatic (and for similar reasons) is the combination of oysters with that legendary aphrodisiac vegetable, asparagus (*see* page 68).

Of course, you don't have to have performance problems to take advantage of sexy soups. Whatever the reason, my advice is the same: eat, drink, and be sexy.

vegetable broth with poached egg

Eggs are the ultimate symbol of fertility. Poached gently in a nutrient-rich stock, they provide much-needed essential ingredients for a night of consuming passion.

6 cups Vegetable Stock (*see* page 13—no bouillon cubes allowed here)

2 large carrots, finely diced

1 small turnip, finely diced

1 large handful of whole fresh herbs, such as sage, thyme, rosemary, and bay leaves

4 eggs

8 sprigs of flat leaf parsley, coarsely chopped

In a large saucepan, bring the stock to simmering point. Add the vegetables and herbs, and boil briskly until reduced by about a quarter—usually 15 minutes.

Strain out the herbs and vegetables, then pour the broth back into the pan.

Place the eggs—still in their shells—in the simmering stock for about 20 seconds (this holds the whites together).

Crack the eggs and poach carefully in the stock until just set—about 4 minutes.

Serve the soup with the eggs floating on top and garnished with the parsley.

Note: you can make this soup several hours before serving. Prepare to the stage at which the eggs have poached, remove them, and place in cold water in the fridge. When ready to serve, put them into the simmering stock for 1 minute and they'll warm up wonderfully.

for a boost of sensual nutrients ...
Eggs supply **protein, iron** and **vitamin E**,
all vital to healthy sexual performance

chilled yogurt and cucumber soup

Throughout Greece and the Middle East, tzatziki—a combination of yogurt, mint, and garlic—is renowned as a potent aphrodisiac. This soup combines those traditional ingredients with a lavish helping of tomato juice.

1 large or 2 small cucumbers, peeled and seeded

2 cups yogurt, preferably plain and probiotic

1¼ cups tomato juice

1 large garlic clove, finely chopped

4 cups cold Vegetable Stock (*see* page 13)

1 large bunch of fresh mint, woody stems removed and leaves finely chopped

1 teaspoon Worcestershire sauce

Slice the cucumber finely and layer it inside a colander, covering each layer with a sprinkle of salt. Leave for 1 hour to allow the excess moisture to run out.

Meanwhile, mix together the yogurt, tomato juice, garlic, stock, and most of the mint.

Tip the cucumber onto a clean dish towel and squeeze out the rest of the moisture. If necessary, chop gently again.

Stir the cucumber into the yogurt mixture.

Serve with a dash of Worcestershire sauce in each bowl and sprinkle with the remaining mint.

for male sexual health ...
Tomatoes are rich in **lycopene**, which is essential for the health of the prostate gland

lettuce, mint, and pea soup

You might find it hard to think of pea soup as sexy, but believe me, this one is. Its wonderfully fresh color conveys a hint of nature and new beginnings. What few people know is that lettuce also contains some amazing mood-enhancing chemicals; in fact, the ancient Greeks used the sap from the cut stems of wild lettuce to make a sleep- and dream-inducing medicine. I don't need to tell you what sort of dreams they were....

5 tablespoon unsalted butter

1 large onion, finely chopped

1 large iceberg lettuce, finely chopped

1 heaping tablespoon flour

5 cups Chicken or Vegetable Stock (*see* page 15 or 13)

3¹⁄₃ cups peas (frozen will do)

1 large bunch of mint, woody stems removed and leaves finely chopped

about 1¼ cups sour cream

In a large saucepan, melt the butter over low heat and gently sweat the onion for 5 minutes.

Add the lettuce and stir until covered with the butter mixture.

Stir in the flour and cook gently for 3–4 minutes.

Add the stock and bring to a boil.

Reduce the heat. Add the peas and most of the mint and simmer until the peas are tender.

Serve with a large spoonful of sour cream on top and sprinkled with the rest of the mint.

to ensure female sexual health ...
Peas are rich in **natural plant hormones** that contribute to female sexuality

thai sweet-and-sour soup

This deliciously light soup is a delight for all the senses. By combining shrimp with the tang of cilantro (which has a long tradition in Asia as an aphrodisiac) and the heady, aromatic oils in lemon grass, you've got a sure-fire winner for a night of passion.

4 cups Fish Stock (*see* page 14)

2-inch piece of lemon grass

2 limes

2 tablespoons honey (preferably organic)

1 handful of chopped cilantro leaves, plus 4 tender sprigs

1lb 2oz shrimp, shelled

In a large saucepan, warm the stock over low heat.

Crush the lemon grass thoroughly.

Juice the limes. Mix the juice with the honey and lemon grass and heat gently with half the stock for 5 minutes.

Remove the lemon grass and pour the honey mixture into the rest of the stock, along with the chopped cilantro.

Simmer for 2 minutes, stirring continuously.

Add the shrimp and poach gently for 5 minutes.

Top each serving with the leaves from the reserved cilantro.

to promote good sexual function ...
Shrimp are rich in **zinc**, vital for the formation of sperm, and **essential fatty acids**, which help maintain fertility

asparagus soup

Of all vegetables, asparagus is regarded as the most potent aphrodisiac, with celery following a pretty close second. Asparagus is one of the oldest of cultivated vegetables and has been grown as food for more than 6000 years. Adding oysters, the most potent of all the aphrodisiac foods, guarantees that this will be the sexiest soup you've ever tasted.

3½ tablespoons unsalted butter

4 large scallions, finely sliced

2 celery sticks, very finely sliced

3 tablespoons flour

5 cups Vegetable Stock (*see* page 13)

1lb 2oz fresh asparagus, trimmed weight (use canned only if you must)

¾ cup plain probiotic yogurt

½ handful of fresh tarragon sprigs

4 shucked oysters

In a large saucepan, melt the butter.

Sweat the scallions and celery gently in the butter for about 5 minutes.

Mix in the flour and stir until the vegetables are well coated.

Pour in the stock and add the asparagus.

Bring to a boil, then simmer until the asparagus is tender—about 8 minutes if fresh, or just to boiling point if canned.

Remove 8 asparagus pieces and set aside.

Process or blend until smooth. Return to a clean saucepan.

Add the yogurt and whisk thoroughly.

Tip in the reserved asparagus pieces and sprigs of tarragon and heat to a simmer.

Serve with the oysters floating on top.

for an aphrodisiac boost ...
Asparagus contains plant hormones called **asparagosides**, which balance hormones and are mildly diuretic
Oysters are rich in **zinc**, which is vital for sexual function

game soup

This is just the soup to get you in the mood for the game of love. Although it might sound rich and heavy, it's actually a very delicate and nourishing broth that is extremely low in fat, very rich in vital sexual nutrients, and enhanced by the sensual aromatic oils in rosemary, sage, and thyme. All game birds are delicious in this recipe.

cooked game carcasses: 1 duck or pheasant, 2 pigeons or other smaller birds, or a combination

2 quarts water

1 large onion, finely chopped

1 large leek, coarsely chopped

2 large celery sticks, chopped

1 large sprig of rosemary

small bunch of parsley

1 large sprig of sage

2 large sprigs of thyme

3 bay leaves

about 1 cup of any root vegetables, cut into strips the size of matchsticks

5 tablespoons port

Put the carcasses into a large saucepan and cover with the water.

Bring to a boil and simmer for about 1 hour.

Add the onion, leek, celery, and herbs.

Bring back to a boil and simmer for 40 minutes.

Strain through kitchen cheesecloth or a fine sieve.

Let cool, then skim off any fat that has risen to the surface.

Add the vegetable strips and simmer until just tender.

Tip in the port and serve.

to supply fortifying essential nutrients ...
Game birds provide **B vitamins**, **natural enzymes**, and **minerals**, all of which promote sexual function and a healthy heart

mussel chowder

All mollusks are renowned as aphrodisiac foods wherever they're eaten. There are as many variations of this recipe as there are zip codes in America, where the famous New England chowder is made with clams. My version uses mussels, which gain added flavor from the bacon.

¼ cup extra virgin olive oil

4 thin slices of unsmoked Canadian bacon, cut into strips

2 large celery sticks, very finely chopped

3 large scallions

2 small potatoes, finely diced

4 cups Fish Stock (*see* page 14)

3 large sprigs of tarragon

3 large sprigs each of parsley, dill, and tarragon, tied together with string

3 bay leaves

about 3¼lb mussels

1 cup dry white wine

1 large handful of flat leaf parsley, finely chopped

In a large saucepan, gently heat half the oil, then sauté the bacon until crisp. Transfer to a plate and set aside.

Add the rest of the oil to the empty pan and add the celery, scallions, and potatoes. Stir to coat thoroughly with the oil and cook gently until soft—about 15 minutes.

Add the stock, tarragon, tied herbs, and bay leaves and simmer for another 10 minutes.

Meanwhile, clean the mussels (discarding any that are already open or broken). Place in a pan with the wine and steam for 10 minutes. Throw out any that don't open. Strain the cooking liquid through cheesecloth and reserve.

When cool enough to handle, remove most of the mussels from their shells, reserving a few whole ones for the garnish, if desired.

Add the shelled mussels and wine to the stock.

Add the reserved bacon and heat gently.

Garnish with the parsley and unshelled mussels, if using.

for a boost of sexual essentials ...
Mussels are rich in **zinc** and **essential fatty acids**
Potatoes supply **vitamin C**

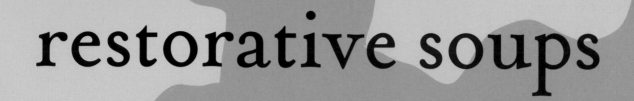

restorative soups

introduction 74

ajo blanco 76

french onion soup 77

brussels sprouts and stilton soup 78

lima bean, parsley, and garlic soup 80

mushroom and bean broth 81

chicken soup with matzo dumplings 82

leek and lentil soup 84

hauser broth 85

Authentic homemade soup certainly lives up to its traditional image in this chapter. It is peasant food at its heartiest, cheapest, and most nourishing—absolutely full of the special nutrients that you crave to restore your body to health, vigor, and vitality.

Included in this chapter are recipes designed specifically for the times when you're stressed by illness, accidents, surgery, trauma, or difficult life events such as death or divorce. During such times, your natural resources become depleted because fighting your way through any unpleasant situation takes an enormous toll on your body's immune defenses and essential stores of nutrients. The object of these recipes is to compensate for any deficiencies, giving you the boost you need to get back to a normal life.

Stimulating a weakened appetite is the first item on any restorative agenda. Even when the thought of food may not appeal, the right soup can still seem appetizing—and it's easy to digest. Believe it or not, the benefits begin to work even before you put that first spoonful to your lips. Just the smell of a pot of soup bubbling away on the stove stimulates the flow of saliva and gastric juices; by the time it's ready, the most jaded of taste buds will have been rekindled, and you'll be ready to take a step on the road to recovery.

Once your appetite has been restored, it's time to address other areas of recuperation. Any form of illness saps both physical and mental strength, and the nutrients you'll find in the following recipes will help restore both. What could be more nourishing, for instance, than a traditional chicken soup such as the one on page 82? With its powerhouse of enzymes and B vitamins, it will help get your mental processes back to peak performance in no time at all. Even the most "high tech" of doctors now admit that chicken soup is good for the body as well as the soul.

When you feel up to stronger flavors, why not try the combination of garlic and almonds on page 76? It's a powerful restorative concoction. The antibacterial, antiviral, and antifungal constituents of garlic provide protection, while the protein, calorie, and mineral content of almonds helps repair damaged cells and provides much-needed energy. In terms of other energy boosters, few foods are better than beans (*see* Lima bean, parsley, and garlic soup, page 80), while the immune-boosting functions of mushrooms have been a staple of folklore for centuries (*see* Mushroom and bean broth, page 81).

I'm always amazed at how many people wrinkle their noses in disgust at the merest mention of Brussels sprouts. While they're certainly not the first food that springs to mind as an appetite stimulant, overlooking them is a major error. When anyone is recovering from an illness, sprouts should be high on the list of recovery foods. They're full of vitamin C, and, like all members of the cabbage family, provide substantial amounts of highly protective and immune-boosting phytochemicals. Combining them with garlic, parsley, celery, and Stilton (*see* page 78) provides a healthy, creamy, and easy-to-eat soup that may well change your view of sprouts for ever.

Of all the commonly used vegetables, the one with the most universal reputation as a restorative is the onion—as much a medicine as it is a food. French onion soup (*see* page 77) is used as a pick-me-up in the street markets of Paris, while in India, ayurvedic medicine (the word means "life knowledge") advocates hot onion dahl to get you back on your feet.

You don't have to be ill to enjoy these delicious soups. They're great at any time and are all just as valuable for good, all-round nutrition.

ajo blanco

This traditional garlic soup of southern Spain provides the extreme healing properties of garlic's sulfur compounds. Combined here with the instant energy derived from natural sugars in the grapes and extra protein from the almonds, the result is a super-restorative bowl of strengthening nutrients.

1½ cups ground almonds

3 tablespoons extra virgin olive oil

4 garlic cloves, very finely chopped

2 cups white bread crumbs

3 cups water

1 cup grape juice

½ cup plain probiotic yogurt

2¼ cups seedless white grapes, halved (and peeled if you can be bothered)

Combine the almonds, oil, and garlic in a bowl and mix thoroughly.

Put into a food processor or blender and add half the bread crumbs, half the water, and half the grape juice.

Blend until completely combined.

Pour into a clean bowl.

Put the rest of the water and grape juice into the processor or blender—no need to rinse it out.

Add the yogurt and pulse about 5 times until combined.

Pour the yogurt mixture into the bread crumb mixture and stir thoroughly.

Leave in the fridge to cool for about 1 hour.

Serve garnished with halved grapes.

for a speedy recovery ...
Garlic is **antibacterial** and **antifungal**
Live yogurt provides **probiotic bacteria** that help restore the immune system

french onion soup

One of the most famous of all restorative soups, this traditional French onion recipe will fill your body with a sense of well-being. It's worth looking for some hard goat cheese, preferably unpasteurized, as it's easy to digest and contains some of the beneficial natural bacteria used in the cheese-making process.

¼ cup extra virgin olive oil

3½ tablespoons butter

4 large onions, finely sliced

6 cups Beef or Vegetable Stock (*see* pages 17 or 13)

1 large handful of mixed parsley, sage, and thyme leaves, finely chopped

3½oz hard goat cheese, shredded

4 × 1-inch slices of a whole-wheat baguette

In a large saucepan, heat the olive oil and butter.

Add the onions and sweat over low heat until thoroughly softened—about 15 minutes.

Add the stock and herbs, reserving some of the sage.

Simmer for about 10 minutes.

Meanwhile, mix the goat cheese with the reserved sage.

Put the cheese mixture onto the bread and broil until the cheese is bubbling.

Serve the soup with the cheesy toast floating on top.

to protect against infection and speed healing ...
Onions contain circulation-boosting **phytochemicals**
Thyme is rich in **thymol**, an antiseptic essential oil
Cheese supplies extra **protein** and **calcium**

brussels sprouts and stilton soup

What a cornucopia of revitalizing, re-energizing, and restorative nutrients! In addition to the benefits of the sprouts, onions, and garlic, this soup contains a gentle cleansing action from the parsley, and lots of bone- and body-building calcium from the Stilton. By the way, it tastes absolutely fabulous, too.

¼ cup extra virgin olive oil

1 large red onion, finely chopped

2 garlic cloves, finely chopped

2 celery sticks, finely chopped

5 cups Vegetable Stock (*see* page 13)

1lb 2oz Brussels sprouts

10½oz Stilton cheese, cubed

1 handful of flat leaf parsley, chopped

Put the olive oil in a large saucepan and place over low heat.

Add the onion, garlic, and celery and sweat gently for 5 minutes.

Add the stock and Brussels sprouts and simmer until the vegetables are tender—about 15 minutes.

Blend until smooth.

Add most of the cheese, return to a simmer and cook until the cheese has melted.

Serve immediately, with the parsley and remaining cheese sprinkled on top.

to revitalize the system ...
Brussels sprouts are rich in cancer-fighting **phytochemicals**
Garlic and onions supply heart-protective and infection-fighting **sulfur compounds**
Olive oil provides healing **vitamin E**

lima bean, parsley, and garlic soup

Lima beans are a favorite in central and southern Europe, as well as in the southern United States. This soup is especially good when made with chicken stock, as it adds more healing enzymes. The vegetable option is almost as effective—it will provide more skin-restoring betacarotene.

¼ cup extra virgin olive oil

1 large onion, finely chopped

2 garlic cloves, finely chopped

6 cups Chicken or Vegetable Stock (*see* page 15 or 13)

2 × 15oz cans lima beans, thoroughly rinsed

2 large handfuls of parsley, very coarsely chopped

In a large saucepan, heat the oil over low heat.

Add the onion and garlic and sweat gently until softened.

Add the rest of the ingredients.

Simmer until the beans are slightly tender—about 15 minutes.

Serve with Herb croutons (*see* page 128).

for a boost of slow-release energy ...
Lima beans are rich in **protein**, **fiber**, **slow-release energy**, **B vitamins**, and **natural plant hormones** that are a valuable aid to women
Parsley is gently **diuretic**

mushroom and bean broth

When your body or mind—or worse still, both—have been through the mill, there's no food quite so physically and emotionally restorative as this interesting broth. The subtle flavor and immune-boosting benefits of mushrooms mix perfectly with the more robust kidney beans to help kick-start the body's regulatory mechanisms.

⅔ cup dried porcini mushrooms

6 cups freshly boiled water

2 celery sticks, coarsely chopped

2 large leeks, chopped

1 large sprig of sage

3 bay leaves

1 × 15oz can kidney beans, thoroughly rinsed

¾ cup plain probiotic yogurt

Soak the mushrooms in the boiling water for 15 minutes.

Strain them, reserving the liquid, and chop coarsely.

Pour the liquid into a large saucepan and bring back to a simmer.

Add the celery, leeks, sage, and bay leaves.

Simmer for another 15 minutes.

Strain again and reserve the liquid.

Add the kidney beans and chopped mushrooms and heat for 10 minutes.

Stir in the yogurt and serve.

to soothe both mind and body ...
Kidney beans are a source of **protein**, **restorative energy**, and **natural plant hormones**
Sage contains **essential oils** that ease digestion and help regulate moods

restorative soups

chicken soup with matzo dumplings

There cannot be a more renowned natural "kitchen medicine" than this traditional Jewish chicken soup. Used as the key to recovery by generations of mothers and grandmothers, it is surprisingly easy to make, and its soothing flavor makes it ideal as a first choice for any recovery program.

7 tablespoons unsalted butter

2 eggs, beaten

4 teaspoons parsley and mint, mixed together

⅔ cup matzo meal

¼ cup warm water

2 quarts Chicken Stock (*see* page 15—no bouillon cubes allowed here)

parsley sprigs, to garnish

Put all the ingredients, except the stock, in a bowl and mix thoroughly.

Leave in the fridge for about 2 hours.

Bring the stock to a gentle simmer.

Roll the refrigerated mixture into 8 equal balls—don't worry if they're very moist.

Drop them into the stock and bring back to a simmer.

Allow to simmer for about 15 minutes.

Serve garnished with the parsley sprigs.

to speed recovery ...
Chicken provides **healing enzymes**, **B vitamins**, and **minerals**
Eggs are rich in **restorative vitamin E**

leek and lentil soup

Like all members of the *Allium* genus of plants, leeks have a long and effective history in the folklore of healing. They've been used as a medicinal food since the time of the ancient Romans, and are valued just as much today. If you're recovering from a cold, flu, or bronchitis, this is the soup to choose.

6 cups Vegetable, Ham, or Beef Stock (see page 13, 16 or 17)

1 cup Puy lentils

1 tablespoon extra virgin olive oil

7oz Canadian bacon, cut into thin shreds

3 large leeks, very finely chopped

2 garlic cloves, finely chopped

1 quantity Matzo dumplings (*see* page 82 or 129)

In a large saucepan, heat the vegetable stock, then pour in the lentils.

Let them cook for about 20 minutes.

Meanwhile, in a separate pan, gently heat the olive oil and sweat the bacon for 5 minutes.

Add the leeks and garlic. Heat very gently until softened.

Once the lentils are tender, add the vegetables and bacon to the stock.

Add the matzo dumplings and simmer for 15 minutes.

to heal throat and chest infections ...
Leeks contain **antibacterial phytochemicals**
Lentils supply easily digested **protein** and essential trace minerals **zinc** and **selenium**

hauser broth

Back in the 1960s I was privileged to meet a fascinating man called Gaylord Hauser, one of the early pioneers of natural medicine and healthy eating in the USA. Today he would be called a guru, as all the great Hollywood stars flocked to him for nutritional advice. He created this recipe as part of his fasting regime, basing it on the cleansing alkaline soups that were part of the traditional European natural-health movement.

¾ cup shredded carrots

1 cup finely chopped celery, with leaves

1 cup spinach, shredded

4 cups water or Vegetable Stock (*see* page 13)

½ cup tomato juice

1 teaspoon honey

1 small handful of chopped parsley or snipped chives, or a mixture of both

Simmer the vegetables in the water or stock for 30 minutes.

Add the tomato juice and honey and cook for 5 minutes.

Blend until smooth.

Serve garnished with the chopped herbs.

to cleanse and heal the system …
Celery and parsley are effective **diuretics**
Carrots contain healing **betacarotene**
Tomatoes are rich in protective **lycopene**

slimming soups

introduction **88**

mixed nettle soup **90**

easy tomato and basil soup **92**

roman spring vegetable soup **93**

jerusalem artichoke soup **94**

dill and turnip soup **96**

celery and brown rice soup **97**

melon and ginger soup **98**

I must admit from the outset that, in principle, I don't advocate extreme slimming diets of any kind. Yes, of course it's true that obesity is a major health problem in the Western world.

In Britain and the USA, obesity currently costs hospital services billions annually for the treatment of related diseases such as diabetes, respiratory illness, arthritis, high blood pressure, and heart disease. The problem robs the British economy of an additional £12 billion in lost productivity, sick pay, welfare, and social care. But this isn't an affliction that can be beaten by quick-fix miracle pills, liposuction, or surgical intervention. The endless advertisements for "light," "low-fat," "lean," "low-cal," "starch-reduced," and similar meaningless but imaginatively named products give you some idea of the size of the market that has been created to feed the gullible fat.

Look closely, however, and you'll see that virtually every product claiming to help you lose weight—whether pill, potion, spread, ready-meal, or snack—carries the neat little phrase "when used as part of a calorie-controlled diet." The truth is that you can lose just as much weight without buying any of these products. Controlling calories isn't the ultimate answer.

What does work is living mostly on a sensible, well-balanced, and varied diet in which at least 50 percent of your energy comes from complex carbohydrates, no more than 30 percent is generated by fat, and around 10 percent is supplied by protein. With few exceptions (and for rare medical reasons), anyone who needs to lose weight can do so by eating a little less and exercising a little more. It's a simple fact that if you cut out 2 slices of bread and butter a day and walk for 15 minutes more, you'll lose 1lb in a week—even if you do nothing else.

In a normal life, there's no room for lunatic dietary regimes such as the cabbage soup diet or the high-protein diet, or diets that depend on the shape of your face or your blood group, diets based on bogus allergy tests that tell you you're fat because you're allergic to wheat or dairy products. The whole meaning of the term "diet" has been debased and changed; used properly, the word describes the normal eating patterns of a nation, or the specific eating habits of different groups of people or of individuals. It should never mean a regime of deprivation, hunger, inadequate nutrition, and misery.

The selection of weight-loss recipes in this chapter is included to provide you with soups that are low in fat—particularly the unhealthiest saturated fats—but that are full of highly nutritious herbs and vegetables. There are dandelion leaves to help stimulate the kidneys and get rid of excess fluid; tomatoes, with their protective lycopene and low calorie content; beans and peas, rich in fiber; protein, essential for growth and repair. Then there are the natural plant hormones that help balance the body's hormone systems: particularly important for women approaching or in the menopause, as they help to stabilize the fluctuations that cause weight gain, hot flashes, and other unpleasant symptoms.

In this chapter you'll find root vegetables such as turnips, another rich source of fiber and minerals, which also give the bulk that makes them filling and satisfying but not fattening. Then there is brown rice, with its mass of B vitamins, followed by stimulating spices such as horseradish and ginger, both of which speed up the circulation and metabolism. I've also included some croutons, a bit of Parmesan cheese, a dollop of rouille, a little butter, and some crème fraîche for a taste of luxury. After all, these recipes, like all the others in this book, have been created for your enjoyment as well as your health.

mixed nettle soup

No, the title isn't a joke. Nettles have been used as a soup-making ingredient for centuries, and form part of a good soup for slimmers. So stop using those highly toxic and dangerous weedkillers and leave space for a clump of nettles and dandelions in your backyard—you'll be doing yourself and the environment a favor. Use gloves to pick the tender, new-grown nettle tips and choose the brightest green leaves from the center of the dandelions for this recipe. The resulting soup will nourish your blood and at the same time help get rid of any puffiness caused by water retention.

2½ cups young stinging nettles, dandelion leaves, arugula, or sorrel (or a mixture of all)

4 tablepoons unsalted butter

4 fat scallions, chopped

¼ cup extra virgin olive oil

5½oz potatoes

5 cups Vegetable Stock (*see* page 13)

1¼ cups low-fat, plain probiotic yogurt

Process the mixed leaves in a food processor or blender.

Soften the butter, mix with the chopped leaves, and put into the fridge.

In a large saucepan, sweat the scallions gently in the oil.

Peel and cube the potatoes and add to the pan. Cook gently for 2 minutes.

Add the stock and simmer for 15 minutes or until the potatoes are cooked.

Stir in the yogurt and blend until smooth.

Return to very low heat, add the leaf mixture, and stir well.

Serve with Herb croutons (*see* page 128).

to help eliminate excess fluid ...
Nettles are rich in **iron** and **vitamin C**
Dandelions are **diuretic**

easy tomato and basil soup

Who today has the time or patience to peel and seed fresh tomatoes? This is my favorite quick-and-easy recipe for homemade tomato soup—without the salt, sugar, and additives found in most commercial varieties. This sustaining and filling soup also boasts natural mood-enhancers.

3 tablespoons canola oil

1 onion, very finely chopped

1 garlic clove, very finely chopped

1 celery stick, finely sliced

2 x 14½oz cans whole plum tomatoes

3 cups Vegetable Stock (*see* page 13)

2 tablespoons tomato paste

12 basil leaves

In a large saucepan, warm the oil over a low heat. Add the onion, garlic, and celery and cook gently for about 5 minutes.

Pour in all the liquid from the cans of tomatoes.

Add the stock and tomato paste and simmer for about 20 minutes.

Slice the tomatoes lengthwise into quarters. Add to the pan with all their juices.

Simmer for another 10 minutes.

Serve with the basil leaves floating on top, or with Floaters made only with basil leaves (*see* page 130).

for a non-fattening, healthy mood boost ...
Celery is **diuretic**
Tomatoes supply cancer-fighting **lycopene**
Basil is rich in mood-enhancing **essential oils**

roman spring vegetable soup

This is "Roman" as in modern, stylish Rome, but similar recipes were used many centuries ago, when the city's inhabitants were already very fond of their soups. A bowl of this makes a sustaining meal, enhanced by the good carbohydrates in pasta and the extra protein and calcium from the cheese.

¼ cup extra virgin olive oil

1 large red onion, finely chopped

3 garlic cloves, very finely chopped

5 cups Vegetable Stock (*see* page 13—no bouillon cubes allowed here)

14oz fresh spring green vegetables, such as green beans, runner beans, peas, or baby fava beans

3½oz conchigliette or any other very small pasta

1 cup grated Parmesan cheese

In a large saucepan, heat the oil and gently sweat the onion for 5 minutes.

Add the garlic and heat for another 3 minutes.

Pour in the stock and bring to a simmer.

Cut the longer vegetables into ½-inch pieces.

Add all the vegetables to the stock and continue simmering.

Depending on which pasta you're using, add it so that the cooking time for the vegetables and pasta coincides.

Serve topped with the grated Parmesan.

to provide a good dose of energy ...
Beans and peas are a great source of **protein**, **fiber**, **slow-release energy**, and **natural plant hormones**

jerusalem artichoke soup

I once tried making Jerusalem artichoke soup and, delicious though it was, I vowed I'd never do it again—those deformed, gnarled little tubers were a nightmare to peel. Now things are different, as there are new varieties that are almost as smooth-skinned as potatoes, but with the distinctive flavor of artichoke. With the added nutritional bonus of crème fraîche, and partnered by a chunk of bread and a small salad, this soup makes a perfect and energizing meal.

2 celery sticks, with leaves

1 large onion, peeled and coarsely chopped

1½lb Jerusalem artichokes, cubed

2 large carrots, cubed

3 bay leaves

6 cups Vegetable Stock (*see* page 13)

1 small handful of chopped chives

¾ cup crème fraîche or sour cream

Cut the leaves off the celery and reserve. Finely slice the celery sticks.

Put all the ingredients, apart from the celery leaves and crème fraîche, into a large saucepan and simmer until the vegetables are soft—about 30 minutes.

Remove the bay leaves and blend or process until smooth.

Return to the pan and stir in the crème fraîche.

Pour into bowls, add a swirl of Rouille (*see* page 129), and serve with the celery leaves floating on top.

Note: if you grow your own chives and are making this soup in the summer, chive flowers make an attractive additional accompaniment perched on top of the rouille.

to improve the digestion …
Jerusalem artichokes are rich in **soluble fiber**, which is extremely satisfying and filling and also improves digestion
Bay leaves contain **essential oils** to help relieve joint pain and improve digestion

dill and turnip soup

This unusual peppery soup is both filling and healthy. Turnips are a storehouse of many vital nutrients which, along with their satisfying texture, makes them a good addition to any weight-loss regime. The health and flavor benefits of parsley and dill are an added bonus in this recipe.

¼ cup canola oil

1 large onion, finely chopped

3 garlic cloves, finely chopped

1lb 2oz young spring turnips, cubed

4 cups Vegetable Stock (*see* page 13)

1 teaspoon dried dill

1 handful of flat leaf parsley, chopped

8 sprigs of fresh dill weed

Heat the oil in a large saucepan and gently sweat the onion and garlic.

Add the turnip cubes and stir until well coated.

Pour in the stock, add the dried dill, and simmer for about 20 minutes.

Blend until smooth.

Bring back to a simmer, add the chopped parsley, and simmer for 5 more minutes.

Serve garnished with the sprigs of fresh dill.

for a low-fat dose of nutrients …
Turnips are high in **fiber**, **calcium**, **phosphorus**, **potassium**, and **B vitamins**
Parsley is gently **diuretic**
Dill helps the **digestive process**

celery and brown rice soup

This makes a great winter soup for anyone fighting the battle of the bulge. Add some good whole-wheat bread, a mixed green salad, and some fresh fruit and you have a nourishing and filling supper. In addition to the benefits of brown rice and horseradish, the betacarotene and minerals in the red pepper and stock make it a worthy slimming soup.

¼ cup extra virgin olive oil

5 thick celery sticks, finely chopped

2 garlic cloves, finely chopped

1 red bell pepper, seeded, and finely chopped

5 cups Vegetable Stock (*see* page 13)

1 cup brown rice

1 teaspoon horseradish sauce

1 handful of flat leaf parsley

Heat the oil in a large saucepan. Add the celery, garlic, and red pepper and heat gently for 5 minutes.

Add the stock and bring to a boil.

Reduce to a simmer and add the rice.

Simmer, covered, until the rice is tender—this could take about 30 minutes (brown rice is much more robust than white).

Check the pot every 10 minutes or so. If it seems to be getting too dry, add more stock or water.

About 5 minutes before the soup is ready, add the horseradish and parsley and stir thoroughly.

for a vitamin and energy boost ...
Brown rice is rich in **fiber**, **B vitamins**, and **slow-release energy**
Horseradish is a general **digestive** and **circulatory stimulant**

melon and ginger soup

Don't make the mistake of serving this too cold or you'll miss out on the delicate flavor. All melons are gently laxative, while mint is one of the best digestive herbs and ginger provides a boost to the metabolism. This is a perfect and refreshing combination if you're trying to lose a few pounds.

1 cantaloupe melon

1 galia melon

1⅔ cup apple juice

2 tablespoons lemon juice

1 bunch of mint, leaves finely chopped, but reserve 4 small sprigs

2 teaspoons ground ginger

Peel, seed, and quarter the melons.

Juice one half of each melon by using a juicer, or by cubing the flesh and pushing it through a fine sieve.

Mix the juiced melon, apple and lemon juice with the chopped mint and ginger.

Leave in a cool place, but not in the fridge, for at least 1 hour.

Use a melon baller or small teaspoon to scoop out the flesh of the reserved melon halves.

Add to the mixed juices.

Serve garnished with the mint sprigs.

for a therapeutic boost of vitamin C ...
Apples provide **vitamin C**, **potassium**, **pectin**, and **malic acid**
Ginger stimulates **circulation**

good-mood soups

introduction 102
spicy parsnip soup 104
sorrel soup 106
pancetta, onion, and green lentil soup 108
smokie soup 109
spicy spinach soup 110

Now, I'm not suggesting that you avoid making the real thing for yourself, but just for a moment, think about all the television advertisements you've seen for soups. The theme that links most of these ads is one of happiness, warmth, and comfort.

The images portrayed show the essence of soup and its ability to create good moods: laughing children with mugs of steaming broth on a cold winter's day; happy families sitting down to a tureen of soup thick enough to stand the ladle in; grandparents smiling in gratitude as a nourishing bowl is placed in front of them. Advertising agencies aren't stupid. They know that, buried deep within our psyche, soup is the type of food that brings joy and comfort to those who consume it.

You might find it hard to believe that what you eat can affect your mood, but cast your mind back to your last hangover and how depressed you felt after drinking too much alcohol. On a more positive note, remember how happy you felt after eating a bar of chocolate. Consider the emotional ups and downs you endure when you don't eat properly. By feeding your irritability with a jam doughnut or pack of cookies, you then find yourself on the roller-coaster ride of wildly fluctuating blood-sugar levels and all the upsetting mood swings that go with them.

What happens to your mood after a wonderful meal with friends or family? How lousy do you feel when you miss breakfast, skip lunch because you're busy and don't get home until 8.30pm? All these emotional fluctuations are related to when you eat, what you eat, and how long you go without eating. Even in the busiest of schedules, there is still time for a bowl of soup. In fact, one of the easiest things to take to work is a vacuum flask full of this homemade good-mood food. Regardless of any underlying medical problems, eating habits play a large role in overall health. Whether the culprit is poor nutrition, erratic eating patterns, or a dependence on high-sugar snacks, sweet canned drinks, or gallons of coffee, whether it surfaces at work, school, or college, or in the hectic life of a busy parent—so many people find themselves limping through everyday tasks, staggering from highs to lows. By the end of the day, just when they should be at their happiest and joining in with friends, families, and partners, these poor souls are at their moodiest and most miserable.

If these scenarios sound all too familiar, don't despair: this chapter was written especially for you. The soups in this section will help smooth out erratic moods because they provide complex carbohydrates, the best source of slow-release energy, which helps keep blood-sugar levels on an even keel. They are also rich in foods containing natural plant chemicals that enhance good moods and lift the spirits, and they're packed full of spices that stimulate both brain and body.

Parsnips, for example—like all the other root vegetables—are a great source of good calories. Green leafy vegetables, such as spinach and sorrel, are rich in iron, which prevents anemia, one of the most common causes of tiredness, irritability, and depression. Oats and lentils are a major source of the B vitamins that are so important in the prevention of depression and the proper functioning of the brain and central nervous system.

Oily fish such as mackerel contains masses of essential fatty acids. These substances are vital for proper brain development in babies and small children, and are known to function as effective anti-inflammatories in both children and adults. These essential fats are also one of the most important constituents of breast milk, but they only get there if there is enough of them in the mother-to-be's diet.

spicy parsnip soup

Parsnips, turnips, and rutabagas are rich sources of slow-release energy, which helps to keep your blood-sugar level on an even keel and prevent mood swings. This soup also gives you a bonus in the form of instant energy from the honey, making it the perfect soup to take to work for a hot, sustaining lunch.

3½ tablespoons unsalted butter

1 large onion, finely sliced

1¼lb mixed parsnips, turnips, celeriac, rutabaga, and potatoes, cubed

3 tablespoons honey

6 cups Vegetable Stock (*see* page 13)

⅔ cup plain probiotic yogurt

2 teaspoons garam masala

In a large saucepan, melt the butter over low heat.

Add the onion and heat gently for 5 minutes.

Add the vegetables and stir to coat well in the butter.

Remove from the heat and drizzle in the honey, stirring to coat all the vegetables.

Pour in the stock and bring to a boil.

Simmer until the vegetables are tender—about 20 minutes.

Blend in a food processor or blender.

Return to the heat.

Stir in the yogurt and garam masala and heat through.

to provide therapeutic energy ...
Parsnips, turnips, and rutabagas are rich sources of **slow-release energy** Garam masala supplies **mood-elevating** spices

sorrel soup

Sorrel isn't used nearly as much as it deserves to be. In addition to its mood-enhancing qualities, this delicious herb also works as an effective detoxifier. This recipe is particularly helpful for those suffering from anxiety, especially when it is associated with insomnia—another common cause of mood swings.

2 large handfuls of sorrel, stripped from the stems

4 tablespoons unsalted butter

4 shallots, peeled and finely sliced

1$\frac{1}{3}$ cups cubed potatoes

5 cups Vegetable Stock (*see* page 13)

1$\frac{2}{3}$ cups plain Greek yogurt

Reserve 8 sorrel leaves and process the rest briefly in a food processor or blender.

In a small saucepan, melt the butter over low heat—don't allow it to smoke or burn.

Mix the processed sorrel into the melted butter and place in the fridge.

Simmer the shallots and potatoes in the stock until tender— about 15 minutes.

Blend the stock mixture until very smooth.

Just before serving, stir in the sorrel and butter mixture and the yogurt. Heat gently.

Serve topped with Potato floaters (*see* page 131).

to soothe and alleviate stressed nerves ...
Sorrel is an excellent source of mood-enhancing **phytochemicals**
Yogurt supplies brain-soothing **tryptophan**

pancetta, onion, and green lentil soup

Like all the legumes, lentils are rich in nutrients that fuel and maintain an even metabolism, which in turn promotes a sense of well-being. These components, together with exceptionally high levels of B vitamins and minerals from the other ingredients, make this a rich and satisfying soup.

¼ cup extra virgin olive oil

1 large onion, very finely diced

5 cups Ham Stock (*see* page 16)

1½ cups green lentils, preferably Puy

9oz pancetta (or unsmoked bacon), rind removed, finely cubed

In a large saucepan, sweat the onion gently in 3 tablespoons of the oil.

Add the stock and bring to a boil.

Pour in the lentils, rinsed if necessary.

Simmer until tender—about 15–25 minutes, depending on the variety of lentils.

About 5 minutes before the soup is ready, fry the pancetta in the remaining oil until crisp.

Drain on paper towels.

Serve the soup sprinkled with the pancetta cubes.

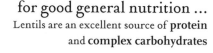

for good general nutrition ...
Lentils are an excellent source of **protein** and **complex carbohydrates**

smokie soup

This unusual combination of oats and smoked mackerel gives a massive mood-boost. In addition to the slow-release energy from the oats and the protein content of the fish, the garlic, leeks, and onion add flavor and loads of protective phytochemicals.

¼ cup extra virgin olive oil

2 large onions, finely chopped

2 leeks, finely chopped

1 garlic clove, finely chopped

1 large carrot, shredded

1 large potato, shredded

2 cups Fish Stock
(*see* page 14)

2 cups water

4 smoked mackerel fillets (not canned), skinned and boned

4 tablespoons unsalted butter

½ cup fine oats

¼ cup heavy cream

In a large saucepan, heat the oil, then sweat the vegetables gently in the oil until soft—about 10–15 minutes.

Add the stock and water and simmer for 15 minutes.

In a separate pan, poach the mackerel fillets with the butter and just enough water to cover them for about 6 minutes.

Pour the poaching liquid into the stock.

Flake the fish, add to the soup, and stir in the oats.

Remove from the heat, cover, and let stand for 10 minutes.

Serve with a spoonful of cream drizzled on each bowl.

to boost energy and mood
Mackerel provides **essential fatty acids**
Oats are rich in **B vitamins** and **soluble fiber**
Olive oil provides **vitamin E**

spicy spinach soup

Here is a valuable, nutritious soup that also promotes a good mood. Spinach mixed with lots of chile and cilantro (both of which have enhanced moods for centuries) turns this soup into a nutritional powerhouse, providing vitamins that help keep both mind and body healthy.

¼ cup extra virgin olive oil

2 red onions, finely chopped

3 garlic cloves, finely sliced

1 teaspoon of seeded and chopped fresh chile

½ handful each of parsley, mint, and cilantro leaves, freshly chopped

1¼lb washed spinach (no need to remove stalks)

6 cups Vegetable Stock (*see* page 13)

¾ cup crème fraîche or sour cream

Heat the oil in a large saucepan and sweat the onions for 2 minutes.

Add the garlic and continue heating for 2 more minutes.

Stir in the chile, parsley, mint, and cilantro and heat for another 2 minutes.

Finely chop the spinach, add to the pan with about 3 tablespoons of the stock, and heat for another 2 minutes, stirring continuously.

Add the rest of the stock and simmer for about 10 minutes.

Stir in the crème fraîche and serve with Emmental croutons (*see* page 128).

to lift the spirits …
Spinach is a rich source of **folic acid**, one of the essential **B vitamins**

winter-warming soups

introduction **114**

thick barley and vegetable soup **116**

luscious mulligatawny **117**

vegetable and bean soup **118**

chickpea and spicy beef sausage soup **120**

spanish bean and chorizo soup **121**

dutch pea soup with smoked sausage **122**

More than any other time of year, winter is the season when we turn naturally to warming soups. During the cold-weather months, your body craves those thick-enough-to-stand-the-spoon-in, rib-sticking, satisfying, and nourishing bowls of homemade goodness.

The soups in this chapter aren't just designed to warm your hands and fill you with energy-giving, heat-generating calories. These recipes will actually help to protect you against winter's ills. An efficient and effective immune system is vital during cold damp months, when viruses thrive and opportunistic bacteria wait for the chance to make their home in your nose, throat, sinuses, chest, or stomach. A great misconception is that food poisoning is mainly a summer ailment; in fact, this is far from true. With central heating running at full tilt and all the windows closed, kitchens are often warmer in winter than they are in summer. People get careless and worry less about putting food into the fridge quickly. Shopping sits around longer before it's unpacked. And when that happens, bacteria have a chance to thrive and multiply.

Seasonal affective disorder (SAD), commonly known as the "winter blues," is another major hazard for many people, and as the days get shorter, their depression gets worse. It might surprise you to know that in addition to the use of antidepressants such as St. John's Wort and exposure to high-intensity light, food is another major factor in the relief of the awful depression that is the main symptom of this condition.

That is why some of the winter-warming soups contain specific nutrients that help overcome the symptoms of SAD. They do this by elevating moods and providing abundant slow-release energy, which helps to keep blood-sugar level on a more even keel. This, in turn, prevents the sudden drop in blood sugar known as hypoglycemia, which is frequently a precursor of a downturn in mood and the start of a depressive episode.

The base for many of these recipes is a variety of root vegetables, all good providers of calories from the complex carbohydrates they contain. They are also a rich source of minerals. Some provide abundant amounts of betacarotene, which the body uses as an antioxidant and protective nutrient, and also converts into vitamin A, which is essential for natural immunity and healthy skin. A vital function of betacarotene is its role in the maintenance of good night vision—so important for anyone driving during winter.

Traditional ingredients of winter soups include all the legumes. Chickpeas, lima beans, fava beans, and split peas are just some of those used in the recipes, and they have unique nutritional properties. They're an excellent source of protein, and of minerals such as calcium, zinc, and even a little iron. They also contain varying amounts of phytoestrogens—natural plant hormones that are particularly important for women.

Not surprisingly, herbs and spices feature in these recipes, too. Curry, bay leaves, chile, and parsley add flavor and warmth. Most important are members of the *Allium* genus of plants: garlic, leeks, and onions. They're antibacterial, antifungal, and antiviral, which means they're hugely protective against virtually all infectious organisms. Their hidden bonus is that they encourage the elimination of cholesterol—especially important during wintertime, when consumption of fatty foods tends to rise. They also help make the blood less sticky and aid in lowering blood pressure.

While all this might sound like a prescription for winter medicine rather than recipes for soups, I assure you that these are the best-tasting prescriptions you'll ever have.

thick barley and vegetable soup

Barley is a staple food in the Middle East, and in ancient Rome was used in soups to feed the gladiators. Sadly, these days it's mostly ignored in Western cooking. This recipe uses wholegrain pot barley, available in most supermarkets and health-food stores, which is a real winter tonic. By contrast, the refined pearl barley provides only calories.

2 tablespoons extra virgin olive oil

1 large onion, finely chopped

1 large carrot, finely cubed

1 large leek, very finely diced

4 cups Vegetable Stock (*see* page 13)

3 bay leaves

5 tablespoons wholegrain pot barley

1 large handful of flat leaf parsley, chopped

In a large saucepan, heat the olive oil. Add the onion, carrot, and leek and heat gently for 5 minutes.

Add the vegetable stock and bay leaves.

Bring to a boil and add the barley.

Simmer for about 1 hour.

Remove the bay leaves.

Serve with the parsley sprinkled on top.

to supply vital nutrients …
Pot barley is rich in **fiber**, **calcium**, **potassium**, and **B vitamins**

luscious mulligatawny

Like many dishes inherited from the days of the Raj—the period of British rule in India—this soup is not only hot, spicy, and warming, but nutritionally valuable as well.

¼ cup extra virgin olive oil

1lb 2oz mixed carrots, leeks, celery, and parsnips, very finely diced

4 plump scallions

2 large garlic cloves, finely chopped

4 teaspoons green curry paste

5 cups Beef Stock (*see* page 17)

juice of 1 mango or ½ cup ready-made mango juice

Heat the oil in a large saucepan. Stir in the vegetables, then cover and sweat for 10 minutes.

Add the curry paste and continue cooking for another 10 minutes, stirring occasionally.

Pour in the stock and simmer until the vegetables are tender.

Add the mango juice and heat through.

Serve with Herb croutons made with cilantro (*see* page 128).

to warm and fortify the consitution ...
Beef stock is rich in **B vitamins**
Leeks, garlic, and onions supply protective **phytochemicals**
Carrots and mango juice provide vital **betacarotene**

vegetable and bean soup

In the middle of winter, you not only need the warming properties of this typical peasant soup, but you'll also benefit from the antibacterial effects of the garlic and onion. A bowlful of this delicious combination will keep you going when you have to shovel the snow away from your door.

¼ cup extra virgin olive oil

1 large onion, very finely chopped

2 garlic cloves, very finely chopped

2 large zucchini, shredded

4 new potatoes, scrubbed and shredded just before use (otherwise they'll discolor)

1 large carrot, shredded

6 cups Vegetable Stock (*see* page 13)

2 cups canned flageolet beans, drained

In a large saucepan, heat the oil. Add the onion and garlic and sweat gently for about 5 minutes.

Add the shredded vegetables and continue heating for 5 more minutes, stirring continuously and adding a little more oil if necessary.

Pour in the stock and simmer for 10 minutes.

Blend in a food processor or blender until smooth.

Return to the pan.

Rinse the beans thoroughly.

Add to the pan, bring back to a simmer, and heat gently for 5 more minutes.

Serve with Rice fritters (*see* page 130).

for a nutritional energy boost ...
Beans and potatoes supply masses of **slow-release energy**
Carrots are rich in immune-boosting **vitamin A**

chickpea and spicy beef sausage soup

This is the perfect soup to choose if you're suffering from the winter blues, because it helps improve everything from circulation to mood. The combination of chickpeas and spicy sausage protects your bones during the dark days of winter, improves blood flow, and promotes balanced blood-sugar levels, lifting the spirits as well as treating the taste buds.

3 tablespoons extra virgin olive oil

1 large onion, finely chopped

½ bulb fennel, finely chopped

1 large head of garlic, finely chopped

10½oz spicy beef sausage, cut into chunks

5 cups Beef Stock (*see* page 17)

2 cups canned chickpeas, rinsed and drained

In a large saucepan, heat the oil. Add the onion, fennel, and garlic and sweat them until softened.

Add the sausage.

Pour in the stock and chickpeas and simmer until tender—about 15 minutes.

Remove ¼ cup of the chickpeas, then blend the rest of the mixture in a food processor or blender.

Return to the heat until boiling.

Serve with the whole chickpeas floating on top.

for all-round nutrition ...
Chickpeas are rich in **calcium**
The beef in the sausages and stock provides **protein**, **iron**, and **B vitamins**, which nourish the nervous system

spanish bean and chorizo soup

Good neighbors can make an enormous difference to your quality of life. My wife, Sally, and I are blessed with the best. Denzil lived for some years in Spain and passed this recipe on to his wife, Vee, who often arrives on our doorstep with a steaming pan of this fabulous taste of Spanish sun to chase away the winter blues.

2 tablespoons extra virgin olive oil

1 onion, finely diced

2 garlic cloves, finely chopped

1 tablespoon all-purpose flour

5 cups Ham Stock (*see* page 16)

2 cups canned lima beans, rinsed

½ cup broad beans

9oz thin chorizo sausage, finely cubed

Heat the olive oil in a large saucepan. Add the onion and garlic and sweat gently until softened—about 10 minutes.

Stir in the flour and continue stirring for about 5 minutes.

Pour in the stock very slowly, stirring until the flour is smoothly incorporated into the liquid.

Add the lima beans and fava beans.

Simmer until the beans are almost tender—about 10 minutes.

Add the chorizo and heat through.

to fight off winter depression ...
Lima beans and fava beans contain **fiber**, **protein**, **minerals**, and **natural plant hormones**, which help elevate mood

dutch pea soup with smoked sausage

Redolent of those wonderful Dutch paintings of frozen winter scenes, this is another of the great peasant recipes of Europe. Split peas give the soup its unique character, and its consistency of thick oatmeal. A bowlful with a chunk of bread and a crisp winter salad is all you need for a nourishing lunch or supper. My dear Dutch friend Henri van der Zee has a pea soup party on his birthday every year—but don't wait a year before you try this recipe for yourself.

1¾ cups split green peas

3 tablespoons unsalted butter

7oz smoked Canadian bacon, finely chopped

1 onion, coarsely chopped

6 cups Ham Stock (*see* page 16)

1lb 2oz good smoked sausage, rind removed and flesh cut into chunks

Soak the peas in plenty of water overnight.

In a large saucepan, melt the butter and sauté the bacon gently for 2 minutes.

Add the onion and continue heating for 4 more minutes.

Stir in the soaked peas, add the stock, and simmer, covered, for 1–2 hours, until the peas are soft.

Mix in the sausage and simmer for another 10–15 minutes.

Note: this robust soup can also be served cold, with any fat skimmed from the top.

for warmth and energy ...
Split peas are rich in **fiber** and **minerals**
Sausage supplies **vital protein**

soup garnishes

introduction **126**

emmental croutons **128**

herb croutons **128**

rouille **129**

matzo dumplings **129**

rice fritters **130**

floaters **130**

potato floaters **131**

zucchini floaters **131**

beet floaters **131**

onion floaters **131**

The function of the garnishes in the following pages is to provide added value to the recipes listed in this book. They help to turn super soups into extra-super soups by adding substance and a bonus of nutrients.

They are all simple to make, too. Once you've grasped the basics, you'll have no trouble in devising your own recipes that include the family's favorite ingredients. Adding the more substantial garnishes, such as dumplings, will turn a simple bowl of soup into a satisfying meal—which is, of course, the historical basis for their inclusion. Dumplings of all sorts are a feature of peasant cooking around the world. From the Russian steppes to the green pastures of rural Ireland, from the Victorian England of Mrs. Beeton to family kitchens in China and Japan, dumplings were the traditional way poor people stretched their limited food supply to fill the stomachs of their hungry families.

In the UK, the usual method for making dumplings is to mix self-rising flour with half the amount of shredded suet, then add salt, pepper, assorted herbs, and just enough water to make a dough firm enough to roll into balls. The *grand'mères* of Brittany in northwest France make their dumplings with buckwheat, which is ideal for those on a gluten-free diet. To make one large dumpling, they combine 4 cups buckwheat flour, a pinch of salt, 4 eggs, a pat of softened butter, 2 tablespoons sugar, lots of black pepper, ⅔ cup milk, and 2 tablespoons each of raisins and chopped prunes with enough water to make a thick batter. Then they wrap it in a dish towel and cook it in the soup.

Japanese cooks are a little more subtle, and their staple rice-flour dumplings are gluten- and wheat-free. Called *dango*, they are made with *shiratamako* (glutinous rice flour). One favorite recipe combines rice flour with cooked, mashed pumpkin and lotus root, which is then rolled into small balls, deep-fried, and tipped into the simmering soup.

In Italy, the favorite garnish is (naturally) pasta. As well as plain pasta, ravioli is often added to soups, and sometimes meatballs make a filling choice. Legend has it that the explorer Marco Polo brought the idea of pasta to Italy from China. True or not, the Chinese certainly make fabulous dumplings from a mixture of mushrooms, bean sprouts, bok choy, ginger, scallions, and eggs wrapped in a flour-and-water dough—very similar to ravioli.

The following dumplings and croutons will make your soups more filling and also add nutritional value. You'll get plenty of calcium, fiber, and B vitamins from Emmental croutons, for example, digestive benefits from essential oils in the Herb croutons, and a little extra iron and protein from Matzo dumplings. Even the simple rouille provides fantastic nutritional qualities. This spicy garlic sauce, traditionally used for fish soup and bouillabaisse, contains masses of vitamin C and betacarotene from the bell pepper, lycopene from the tomatoes, heart protection from the garlic, cancer-fighting properties from the turmeric, and some vitamin E for skin and circulation from the olive oil.

The floater recipes might sound odd, but my wife and I devised these as a simple, delicious way of adding body and nutrients to any soup. Onion floaters will help with any form of cold, cough, or chest infection. Use the Beet floaters for anyone with anemia, or after surgery, when there may have been blood loss; they're great for women, too, especially just before, during and after periods. The thyme in the Potato floaters adds antiseptic value to the extra energy they supply, while the Zucchini floaters contain betacarotene.

Use the following recipes, but be inventive with your own too, and you'll get even more super nutrients from my super soups.

emmental croutons

Add to clear soups for extra calcium and protein, as well as the nutrients in the whole-wheat bread.

2 tablespoons extra virgin olive oil

4 slices of stale whole-wheat bread

4½oz Emmental cheese

In a skillet, heat the oil until slightly smoking.

Remove the crusts from the bread and cut what remains into ½-inch cubes.

Grate the cheese finely.

Roll the bread in the cheese, pressing it in firmly.

Fry in the oil, turning continuously, until golden on all sides.

herb croutons

Use different herbs for their specific properties.

1⅔ cups whole-wheat bread crumbs

2 teaspoons fresh, soft herbs such as mint, parsley, sorrel, cilantro, basil (not tough ones such as rosemary), finely chopped

1 small egg, whisked

3 tablespoons extra virgin olive oil

Mix the bread crumbs with the herbs.

Form into small balls about the size of an acorn, then flatten with your hands.

Dip into the egg and drain.

In a skillet, heat the oil until smoking slightly.

Fry the eggy bread balls until slightly golden—about 2 minutes.

rouille

Not just the delicious traditional French essential for fish soup, but a garnish bursting with heart-protective, cancer-fighting lycopene, garlic, and turmeric.

½ red bell pepper, peeled and seeded

½ cup canned tomatoes, drained of most liquid

3 garlic cloves, peeled

2 thick slices of whole-wheat bread, soaked in water

1 teaspoon ground turmeric

5 tablespoons extra virgin olive oil

Process the pepper, tomatoes, and garlic in a food processor or blender.

Add the bread and process again.

Whisk the turmeric into the olive oil.

Pour the olive oil mixture gradually into the food processor or blender, pulsing until smooth.

matzo dumplings

These contain good carbohydrates, energy, and extra nutrients. Use them to turn your soup into a more sustaining meal.

7 tablespoons unsalted butter

2 eggs, beaten

2 teaspoons each chopped parsley and mint

⅔ cup matzo meal

¼ cup warm water

Mix all the ingredients thoroughly in a bowl. Leave in the fridge for about 2 hours.

Roll the mix into 8 balls—don't worry if they're very moist.

Drop them into the soup. Bring back to a simmer and let them cook for about 15 minutes.

rice fritters

Give additional protein, calcium, iron, and B vitamins to any soup with these fritters.

1 large egg

¾ cup cooked rice (leftovers are perfect)

4 tablespoons grated Parmesan cheese

1 tablespoon chopped soft herbs such as parsley, sage, tarragon

1¾ sticks unsalted butter

Beat the egg.

Mix the rice with the cheese and stir in enough egg to make it stick together.

Add the herbs and mix thoroughly again.

Put the mixture into your palms and roll until gooey.

Divide into small balls. Flatten until they're about 1 inch across.

Leave in the fridge for 1 hour.

Melt the butter in a skillet. Fry the fritters for about 5 minutes on each side.

floaters

This is the basic recipe to which you can add your own ideas. Any herbs you add must be soft such as parsley, sage, mint, and tarragon—not woody like rosemary.

1¼ cups whole-wheat flour

1 egg , whisked

2 twists of freshly ground black pepper

vegetables (*see* page 131)

6 tablespoons extra virgin olive oil

Beat the flour into the egg. Add the pepper.

Shred the vegetables to be used. Squeeze out as much water as possible, squash them into walnut-size balls, then flatten until they're about ½ inch thick.

Coat them in the batter mixture. Heat the oil and gently sauté the floaters for 3 minutes on each side.

potato floaters

Use about 3½oz baking potato flesh; be sure to rinse after shredding to get rid of the starch. Add 1 tablespoon freshly chopped thyme. Potatoes are a good source of extra vitamin C. Thymol, the essential oil in thyme, is a powerful antibacterial.

zucchini floaters

Use about 7oz unpeeled zucchini. Add 3 tablespoons chopped flat leaf parsley. Extra betacarotene from the zucchini skin, combined with the gentle diuretic effect of parsley, makes these floaters good for skin problems.

beet floaters

Use ⅔ cup freshly shredded raw beet mixed with 1 teaspoon horseradish. One of the best blood boosters, beets are used in eastern Europe to treat anemia.

onion floaters

Use 1 *very* finely grated onion, or 3 large grated scallions, with 2 teaspoons chopped fresh oregano. Choose these for extra protection against infections, coughs, and colds, and for the mood-boosting and antiseptic properties of oregano.

soup healing

introduction 134
soup healing charts 136

If I've learned one thing after nearly 40 years of working with patients, 25 years presenting *BodyTalk*, a radio phone-in show and 20 years answering readers' questions in newspapers and magazines, it's that the general population has an enormous thirst for knowledge.

Amazingly, I'm still being asked questions that, in all these years, have never been asked before. But whatever the questions, they nearly all have one thing in common. When ordinary men, women, mothers, fathers, grandparents (and growing numbers of children and teenagers) phone in or write, they're looking for help with an illness or an explanation of a symptom. That's the reason I've included the healing charts (*see* pages 136–40) in *Super Soups*. I'm certain that many of you looking at this book for the first time will have turned straight to this section to see if there is a remedy for your specific problem. If the pharmacy is your first port of call for the relief of minor ailments, it may come as a surprise that there could be healing benefits in a bowl of soup. Older readers, however, may well remember their grandmothers' reliance on these and other traditional "kitchen remedies."

As a naturopath, I've embraced kitchen medicine as part of my philosophy since my college days. It is a branch of medicine based on principles that stretch back to the earliest beginnings of the human race. In fact, the whole ethos of "food as medicine" grew out of the use of herbs and plants by medicine men and witchdoctors. It is found in religious teachings, such as those of the priests of antiquity in Egypt, the earliest monks and nuns of Christianity, the ancient traditions of ayurveda in India, and the healing mystics of the Jewish cabbala. It also appears in the wonders of Tibetan medicine and the medicinal foods of traditional Chinese medicine. This common principle was encapsulated in the words of Hippocrates, the father of modern medicine, when he wrote: "Man should let his food be his medicine, and his medicine be his food." So, if this is your first venture into using foods to heal, you are joining a long, ancient, and worthy tradition.

Food provides your body with the essential protein, fats, carbohydrates, vitamins, and minerals it needs to survive. But food consists of much more than these basic nutrients. Plants, for example, contain hundreds of natural chemical substances, many of which have specific therapeutic benefits. In earlier times, people discovered these benefits by chance, and the value of particular plants was taught and handed down from generation to generation. No one knew why onion or garlic soothed a cough, for example, or liver and carrots could make you see in the dark, but they made use of that knowledge. No one understood the reasons why mint relieved indigestion, shellfish made men feel sexy, or lettuce helped induce sleep; they simply used this knowledge and passed it on. In this book I pass it on to you.

Happily, in the 21st century there has been a massive increase in interest in the medicinal properties of food. Hardly a week goes by without the publication of new research in the world's leading medical journals, where we can read that tomatoes help control prostate cancer, wholegrain cereals prevent heart disease, garlic lowers cholesterol, oily fish improves brain development in babies and reduces the pain of arthritis... the list is almost endless.

So whatever your health problem, there will surely be a herb, spice, or foodstuff that can help. Some will reduce the severity of symptoms, others will protect against degenerative diseases, and still others could prevent a recurrence of distressing or even life-threatening conditions.

soup healing charts

condition	healing foods	effect
Acne	Cabbage	Is rich in antiobiotic sulfur compounds
	Fennel	Improves fat digestion
	Garlic, onions	Are antibacterial
Anemia	Nettles, watercress	Are rich in iron and the vitamin C required for iron absorption
	Red meat	All red meats contain easily absorbed iron
Anxiety	Basil, rosemary	Contain calming essential oils
	Bread, dairy products	Encourage the brain's production of feel-good hormones
Arthritis	Oily fish	Essential fatty acids in oily fish are natural anti-inflammatories
	Celery	Eliminates uric acid
	Broccoli, turnips	Supply protective antioxidants
Asthma	Garlic, onions, leeks	Are natural decongestants
	Watercress	Is rich in unique lung protective chemicals
	Olive oil	Provides vitamin E—essential for healthy lung tissue
Back pain	Thyme	Is a muscle-relaxant
	Oily fish, mussels	Provide natural anti-inflammatories
	Chiles, curry	Stimulate blood flow and speed healing
Bronchitis	Garlic, onions, leeks	Are powerful antibacterials and decongestants
	Cilantro, thyme	Are expectorant and decongestant
Catarrh	Garlic, onions, leeks	Are powerful antibacterials and decongestants
	Citlantro, thyme	Are expectorant and decongestant
Chilblains	Sorrel, basil, garlic, cilantro, chile	All these herbs and spices help improve the circulation

condition	healing foods	effect
Cholesterol	Garlic, onions, leeks, chives	All, especially garlic, help lower cholesterol
	Oats, beans	Provide special fiber, which also reduces cholesterol levels
Chronic fatigue	Basil, bay, sage	All are mood-enhancing
	Beans, lentils, barley, oats, rice, bread	Beans and cereals provide good energy
	Eggs, meat, fish, poultry	All are needed for protein
Circulation problems	Sorrel, basil, garlic, cilantro, chile	All these herbs and spices help improve the circulation
Colds	Garlic, onions, leeks	Are decongestant and protect against secondary infections
	Chives, thyme, sage, rosemary	Essential oils in these herbs are antiviral
	Shellfish	Contain immune-boosting zinc
Constipation	Nettles, sorrel	Are gentle laxatives
	Beans, lentils, oats, barley	Are rich sources of fiber, which improves colonic function
Cough	Garlic, onions, leeks	Are powerful antibacterials and decongestants
	Cilantro, thyme	Are expectorant and decongestant
Cystitis	Garlic	Is antibacterial and antifungal
	Celery, parsley	Both are gentle, cleansing diuretics
Depression	Basil, rosemary	Are mood-enhancers
	Oats, red meat, beans, lentils	All are excellent sources of B vitamins, essential for the nervous system
Diarrhea	Mint	Soothes the digestive tract
	Garlic	Helps fight any food-poisoning bacteria
	Rice, carrots	Are easily digested and non-irritant
Diverticulitis	Garlic	Helps prevent infection
	Mint	Soothes the digestive tract
	Rice, carrots	Are easily digested and non-irritant

condition	healing foods	effect
Flatulence	Fennel, mint, cilantro	All contain essential volatile oils, which improve digestion and reduce flatulence
Fluid retention	Parsley	Is one of the most effective natural diuretics. Use generously
	Celery	Is a gentle diuretic
Gallstones	Sage, fennel, tarragon	All aid fat digestion and reduce stone-causing cholesterol
	Parsnips, turnips, brown rice, oats	Are excellent sources of soluble fiber, which speeds the removal of cholesterol
Gingivitis	Cherries, tomatoes	Are rich in immune-boosting vitamin C
	Thyme	Is a powerful antiseptic
	Shrimp	Provide zinc, essential for good resistance
Gout	Celery, parsley, turnips	All reduce levels of uric acid
	Nasturtium flowers	Contain mustard oils, which relieve pain
	Shellfish	Help reduce inflammation
Hair problems	Bok choy	Contains sulfur and vitamin C
	Nettles, rosemary	Both are antiseptic (good in shampoos, too)
	Meat, poultry	Provide iron and B vitamins
	Fish, shellfish	Provide iodine for thyroid function, often a factor in hair problems
Headache	Dandelion leaves	Are diuretic, helping to relieve headaches caused by fluid retention
	Rosemary, mint	Are mood-altering herbs that help stress-related headaches
	Garam masala, curry, chile	Improve blood-flow to the brain for the relief of migraines
	Barley, potatoes	Contain starch, which keeps blood sugar on an even keel
Heartburn	Mint, dill weed	Contain natural antacid essential oils
	Yogurt	Provides good bacteria, which aid digestion
	Rice, carrots	Are traditional naturopathic foods for all digestive upsets

condition	healing foods	effect
Heart disease	Garlic	Helps reduce cholesterol, blood pressure, and the risk of clots
	Ginger, chile, curry	Stimulate circulation
	Beans, wholegrain cereals	Reduce cholesterol
	Oily fish	Is cardio-protective
Hepatitis	Artichokes	Are a source of cynarin, which helps liver function
	Sage, tarragon, horseradish	All improve fat digestion
Herpes	Garlic, leeks	Both are traditional remedies for herpes and are believed to contain antiviral substances
Hypertension	Garlic	Phytochemicals in garlic are beneficial to good blood pressure
	Parsley, celery	Reduce fluid retention
	Wholegrain cereals	Help control cholesterol, often a factor in hypertension
Indigestion	Mint, dill weed, fennel	All help improve digestion thanks to their essential oils
	Carrots, sweet potatoes	Both are rich in healing betacarotenes
	Yogurt	Improves digestion and prevents flatulence
Influenza	Chicken soup	The traditional flu healer, rich in protein and protective enzymes
	Ginger, turmeric, chile	Speed the elimination of toxins
	Wholegrain cereals	Provide B vitamins to prevent post-flu depression
Insomnia	Lettuce	Contains mildly soporific chemicals
	Basil	Is wonderfully calming
	Milk, yogurt, fromage frais, crème fraîche, poultry, oily fish	All supply sleep-inducing tryptophans

condition	healing foods	effect
Laryngitis	Sage, rosemary	Contain essential oils that are specifically antibacterial to the bugs that commonly cause throat problems
Menstrual problems	Sorrel, nettles	Provide iron to prevent anemia
	Celery, parsley	Ease uncomfortable fluid retention
	Oily fish	Is anti-inflammatory, for pain relief
	Cherries	Are rich in potassium
	Beans	Are a source of phytoestrogens, which reduce hormonal fluctuations
Mouth ulcers	Garlic	Helps with healing
	Yogurt	Contains good bacteria that helps to prevent ulcers
	Basil, rosemary, pasta, rice, bread, potatoes	Are all stress-relievers: important as ulcers are mostly stress-induced
Obesity	Most of the super soups	Good soups are filling and sustaining as they provide slow-release energy, which prevents fluctuations in blood sugar and food cravings
Raynaud's syndrome	Basil, sorrel, cilantro, garlic, chile	All help improve the circulation
Restless legs	Watercress, nettles, red meat, green leafy vegetables	Contain iron to prevent anemia, a common cause of this condition
SAD (winter blues)	Basil, rosemary	Both contain mood-enhancing essential oils
	Oats	Are rich in antidepressant B vitamins
	Starchy foods	Increase levels of mood-enhancing tryptophan
Sinusitis	Onions, garlic, leeks	Are powerful antibacterials and decongestants
	Cilantro, thyme	Both are expectorant and decongestant
Varicose veins	Ginger, chile, curry powder, garam masala	All stimulate and improve circulation
	Broccoli	Is a rich source of vein-protecting betacarotene and other antioxidants
	Lentils, beans, barley, oats	All prevent constipation, a common cause of varicose veins

index

acne 48, 136
ajo blanco 76
almonds
  ajo blanco 76
  carrot and almond cream 51
  health benefits of 75
anemia 103, 127, 131, 136
antibacterial mustard oils 56
antioxidants 20, 21
anxiety 136
aphrodisiac foods 61
apple juice
  melon and ginger soup 98
arthritis 135, 136
asparagus 61
  asparagus soup 68
asthma 136
ayurvedic medicine 75, 134

back pain 136
bacon
  Dutch pea soup with smoked sausage 122
  leek and lentil soup 84
  mussel chowder 71
barley
  thick barley and vegetable soup 116
basil
  easy tomato and basil soup 92
bay leaves 21, 94
beans
  curried parsnip and vegetable soup 38
  health benefits of 115, 121
  lima bean, parsley, and garlic soup 80
  mushroom and bean broth 75, 81
  Roman spring vegetable soup 93
  Spanish bean and chorizo soup 121
  vegetable and bean soup 118
  Welsh minestrone with rice and leeks 27
beef stock 17
beets
  beet floaters 127, 131
  beet soup 41
  health benefits of 34–5, 41
bell peppers
  celery and brown rice soup 97
  rouille 23, 129
betacarotene 22, 42, 43, 52, 56, 80, 115
bioflavonoids 35
Blanc, Raymond 10
blood-sugar levels 102, 103, 114

bok choy
  Chinese bok choy and chicken soup 24
bread
  bread and garlic soup 26
  Emmental croutons 127, 128
  herb croutons 127, 128
  rouille 129
broccoli
  oat and broccoli soup 42
bronchitis 136
Brussels sprouts 75
  Brussels sprouts and Stilton soup 75, 78
buckwheat dumplings 126

cabbage 21
  cabbage soup with ham 28
calcium 115
cancer 135
carotenoids 21
carrots
  beef stock 17
  beet soup 41
  carrot and almond cream 51
  duck soup with prunes 31
  fish stock 14
  ginger, leek, and carrot soup 39
  ham stock 16
  hauser broth 85
  health benefits of 51
  Jerusalem artichoke soup 94
  luscious mulligatawny 117
  oxtail soup 43
  smokie soup 109
  spicy carrot and orange soup 54
  thick barley and vegetable soup 116
  vegetable and bean soup 118
  vegetable broth with poached egg 62
  vegetable stock 13
catarrh 136
celery
  beef stock 17
  Brussels sprouts and Stilton soup 78
  celery and brown rice soup 97
  chicken stock 15
  duck soup with prunes 31
  easy tomato and basil soup 92
  game soup 69
  ham stock 16
  hauser broth 85
  Jerusalem artichoke soup 94

luscious mulligatawny 117
mushroom and bean broth 81
mussel chowder 71
vegetable stock 13
chard
  chicken, chile, chard, and noodle soup 30
cheese
  Brussels sprouts and Stilton soup 78
  Emmental croutons 127, 128
  French onion soup 75, 77
  rice fritters 130
  Roman spring vegetable soup 93
cherries 35
  sweet cherry soup 44
chest infections 84
chicken
  chicken soup with matzo dumplings 74, 82
  Chinese bok choy and chicken soup 24
  chicken stock 15
  chicken, chile, chard, and noodle soup 30
chickpeas 115, 120
  chickpea and spicy beef sausage soup 120
chilblains 136
chiles 21, 36
  chicken, chile, chard, and noodle soup 30
  Chinese dumplings 127
  Chinese bok choy and chicken soup 24
cholesterol 35, 115, 135, 137
chorizo
  Spanish bean and chorizo soup 121
chronic fatigue 137
cilantro
  spicy spinach soup 110
circulation problems 34–5, 137
coconut milk
  spiced lentil soup 36–7
colds 137
constipation 137
corn and smoked haddock chowder 55
coughs 137
cranberry juice
  sweet cherry soup 44
croutons 127
  Emmental croutons 127, 128
  herb croutons 127, 128
cucumber
  chilled yogurt and cucumber soup 64
  curried parsnip and vegetable soup 38
cystitis 137

dandelion leaves 89
  mixed nettle soup 90
depression 102, 103
  healing foods for 137
  SAD (seasonal affective disorder) 114
diarrhea 137
diets 88–9
dill and turnip soup 96
diverticulitis 137
duck soup with prunes 31
dumplings 126–7
  matzo dumplings 127, 129
  chicken soup with matzo dumplings 82
  leek and lentil soup 84
Dutch pea soup with smoked sausage 122

eczema 48, 49
eggs 61
  vegetable broth with poached egg 62
Emmental croutons 127, 128
essential fatty acids 103

fennel..50
  chickpea and spicy beef sausage soup 120
  iced fennel soup 50
fertility problems 60
fish stock 14
flatulence 138
floaters 127, 130–1
  beet 127, 131
  onion 127, 131
  potato 23, 127, 131
  zucchini 127, 131
Florence fennel 50
fluid retention 138
folic acid 56
French onion soup 75, 77

gadgets 11
gallstones 138
game soup 69
garlic
  ajo blanco 76
  bread and garlic soup 26
  Brussels sprouts and Stilton soup 78
  celery and brown rice soup 97
  chickpea and spicy beef sausage soup 120
  dill and turnip soup 96
  easy tomato and basil soup 92
  health benefits of 21, 35, 75, 115
  lima bean, parsley, and garlic soup 80
  Roman spring vegetable soup 93
  rouille 23, 129
  spicy spinach soup 110
  sweet potato and garlic soup 52
  vegetable and bean soup 118

ginger
  ginger, leek and carrot soup 39
  melon and ginger soup 98
  spicy carrot and orange soup 54
gingerole 36, 49
gingivitis 138
gout 138
grapes
  ajo blanco 76

hair problems 138
ham
  cabbage soup with ham 28
ham stock 16
hauser broth 85
Hauser, Gaylord 85
headaches 138
heart disease 135, 139
heartburn 138
hepatitis 139
herb croutons 127, 128
herbs 10, 21, 115
  floaters 130
  rice fritters 130
herpes 139
Hippocrates 134 5
honey
  hauser broth 85
  spicy parsnip soup 104
  Thai sweet-and-sour soup 66
horseradish
  beet floaters 131
  celery and brown rice soup 97
hypertension 139
hypoglycemia 114

iced fennel soup 50
India
  ayurvedic medicine 75, 134
indigestion 139
influenza 139
insomnia 139
iodine 55
iron 103, 115

Japanese rice flour dumplings 126–7
Jerusalem artichoke soup 94

laryngitis 140
leeks
  beef stock 17
  chicken stock 15
  fish stock 14
  game soup 69
  ginger, leek, and carrot soup 39
  ham stock 16

health benefits of 21, 35, 39, 115
leek and lentil soup 84
luscious mulligatawny 117
mushroom and bean broth 81
smokie soup 109
thick barley and vegetable soup 116
vegetable stock 13
Welsh minestrone with rice and leeks 27
lemon grass
  Thai sweet-and-sour soup 66
lentils
  health benefits of 35, 103
  leek and lentil soup 84
  pancetta, onion, and green lentil soup 108
  spiced lentil soup 36
lettuce, mint, and pea soup 65
lima bean, parsley, and garlic soup 80
luscious mulligatawny 117
lycopene 64

mackerel 103
  smokie soup 109
mango juice
  luscious mulligatawny 117
Marco Polo 127
matzo dumplings 127, 129
  chicken soup with matzo dumplings 82
  leek and lentil soup 84
medicine, soup as 20–1, 134–5
melon and ginger soup 98
menopause 89
menstrual problems 127, 140
mint
  chicken soup with matzo dumplings 82
  lettuce, mint, and pea soup 65
  matzo dumplings 127, 129
  melon and ginger soup 98
  spicy spinach soup 110
mixed nettle soup 90
mood swings 102, 103, 106
mouth ulcers 140
mulligatawny, luscious 117
mushroom and bean broth 75, 81
mussel chowder 61, 71

nasturtiums
  pumpkin soup with nasturtium flowers 56
nettles
  mixed nettle soup 90
noodles
  cabbage soup with ham 28
  chicken, chile, chard, and noodle soup 30
oats
  health benefits of 42, 103
  oat and broccoli soup 42
  smokie soup 109

obesity 88, 140
oily fish 103
onions
  Brussels sprouts and Stilton soup 78
  French onion soup 75, 77
  health benefits of 21, 34, 35, 75, 115
  onion floaters 127, 131
  pancetta, onion, and green lentil soup 108
  Roman spring vegetable soup 93
  thick barley and vegetable soup 116
  vegetable and bean soup 118
  white onion soup 23
orange juice
  spicy carrot and orange soup 54
oregano 21
  onion floaters 131
oxtail soup 43
oysters 61
  asparagus soup 68

pancetta, onion, and green lentil soup 108
pantry 10
parsley
  chicken soup with matzo dumplings 82
  lima bean, parsley, and garlic soup 80
  matzo dumplings 127, 129
  spicy spinach soup 110
  white onion soup 23
  zucchini floaters 131
parsnips
  curried parsnip and vegetable soup 38
  health benefits of 103
  luscious mulligatawny 117
  spicy parsnip soup 104
  vegetable stock 13
pasta 127
peas
  curried parsnip and vegetable soup 38
  health benefits of 65
  lettuce, mint, and pea soup 65
  Roman spring vegetable soup 93
  Welsh minestrone with rice and leeks 27

phytochemicals 20, 21, 22, 35, 51
phytoestrogens 115
potatoes
  cabbage soup with ham 28
  iced fennel soup 50
  mixed nettle soup 90
  mussel chowder 71
  potato floaters 23, 127, 131
  spicy parsnip soup 104
  vegetable and bean soup 118

prostate cancer 135
prunes 21

duck soup with prunes 31
psoriasis 48, 49
pumpkin soup with nasturtium flowers 56

Raynaud's syndrome 34, 140
restless legs 140
rice 89
  celery and brown rice soup 97
  rice fritters 130
  Welsh minestrone with rice and leeks 27
rice flour
  Japanese rice flour dumplings 126–7
Roman spring vegetable soup 93
rosemary 21
  white onion soup 23
rouille 23, 129
rutabagas
  oxtail soup 43
  spicy parsnip soup 104

SAD (seasonal affective disorder) 114, 140
St. John's Wort 114
sausages
  chickpea and spicy beef sausage soup 120
  Dutch pea soup with smoked sausage 122
  Spanish bean and chorizo soup 121
seasonal affective disorder (SAD) 114, 140
scallions
  mixed nettle soup 90
sexual problems 60 1
shrimp
  Thai sweet-and-sour soup 61, 66
sinusitis 140
skin disorders 48 9
smoked haddock
  sweetcorn and smoked haddock chowder 55
smoked sausage
  Dutch pea soup with smoked sausage 122
soluble fiber 94
sorrel 103
  sorrel soup 106
spices 21, 35, 115
  spiced lentil soup 36–7
  spicy parsnip soup 104
spinach 103
  hauser broth 85
  spicy spinach soup 110
split peas 115
  Dutch pea soup with smoked sausage 122
stocks 12–17
  beef 17
  bouillon cubes 12
  chicken 15
  fish 14
  freezing 12
  ham 16

using with water 12
  vegetable 13
sweet cherry soup 44
sweet potatoes
  sweet potato and garlic soup 52

Thai sweet-and-sour soup 66
throat infections 84
thyme
  potato floaters 127, 131
  white onion soup 23
tomato juice
  chilled yogurt and cucumber soup 64
  hauser broth 85
tomatoes
  easy tomato and basil soup 92
  health benefits of 64, 135
  rouille 23, 129
turnips 89
  dill and turnip soup 96
  oxtail soup 43
  spicy parsnip soup 104
  vegetable broth with poached egg 62
tzatziki 64

varicose veins 140
vegetable broth with poached egg 62
vegetable stock 13
vitamins
  B vitamins 103
  vitamin A 115
  vitamin E 49, 52, 127

watercress
  creamy watercress soup 22
  Welsh minestrone with rice and leeks 27
white onion soup 23
winter blues (SAD) 114, 140

yogurt
  ajo blanco 76
  beet soup 41
  chilled yogurt and cucumber soup 64
  creamy watercress soup 22
  mixed nettle soup 90
  mushroom and bean broth 81
  spicy parsnip soup 104

zinc 66, 68, 71, 115
zucchini
  zucchini floaters 127, 131
  vegetable and bean soup 118

acknowledgments for the first edition

As always, I have to thank my wife, Sally, who spent many hours with her head over an endless succession of steaming saucepans developing these delicious recipes. I must also thank Jamie Ambrose for patiently editing yet another of my books—and especially Lara Maiklem and Hilary Lumsden at Mitchell Beazley for not getting angry when my e-mails didn't get through. Special thanks go to Nicki Dowey for her excellent and imaginative photography and the design team for their creative input.